Modern Constitutions

K. C. WHEARE

Modern Constitutions

London

OXFORD UNIVERSITY PRESS

New York Toronto

Oxford University Press, Ely House, London W. 1

GLASGOW   NEW YORK   TORONTO   MELBOURNE   WELLINGTON
CAPE TOWN   IBADAN   NAIROBI   DAR ES SALAAM   LUSAKA   ADDIS ABABA
DELHI   BOMBAY   CALCUTTA   MADRAS   KARACHI   LAHORE   DACCA
KUALA LUMPUR   SINGAPORE   HONG KONG   TOKYO

JF
71
. W3
1966

First published in the Home University Library *1951*
Second edition first published as an Oxford University Press paperback 1966

REPRINTED LITHOGRAPHICALLY IN GREAT BRITAIN
FROM CORRECTED SHEETS OF THE SECOND EDITION
AT THE UNIVERSITY PRESS, OXFORD
BY VIVIAN RIDLER, PRINTER TO THE UNIVERSITY
1971

Contents

1
What a Constitution Is

THE WORD 'constitution' is commonly used in at least two senses in any ordinary discussion of political affairs. First of all it is used to describe the whole system of government of a country, the collection of rules which establish and regulate or govern the government. These rules are partly legal, in the sense that courts of law will recognize and apply them, and partly non-legal or extra-legal, taking the form of usages, understandings, customs, or conventions which courts do not recognize as law but which are not less effective in regulating the government than the rules of law strictly so called.

In most countries of the world the system of government is composed of this mixture of legal and non-legal rules and it is possible to speak of this collection of rules as 'the Constitution'. Indeed when we speak of the English or the British Constitution this is the normal, if not the only possible, meaning which the word has. The British Constitution is the collection of legal rules and non-legal rules which govern the government in Britain. The legal rules are embodied in statutes like the Act of Settlement which regulates the succession to the throne, the various Representation of the People Acts which since 1832 have introduced by stages the universal franchise, the Judicature Acts, and the Parliament Acts of 1911 and 1949 which restricted the powers of the House of Lords. They may also be found in orders and regulations issued under the prerogative or under statutory authority; and they may be embodied in the decisions of courts. The non-legal rules find expression in such customs or conventions as that the Queen does not refuse her assent

A*

to a bill duly passed by Lords and Commons or that a Prime Minister holds office because and for so long as he retains the confidence of a majority in the House of Commons. All these rules are part of the British Constitution.

In almost every country in the world except Britain, however, the word 'constitution' is used in a narrower sense than this. It is used to describe not the whole collection of rules, legal and non-legal, but rather a selection of them which has usually been embodied in one document or in a few closely related documents. What is more, this selection is almost invariably a selection of legal rules only. 'The Constitution', then, for most countries in the world, is a selection of the legal rules which govern the government of that country and which have been embodied in a document.

Perhaps the most famous example of a Constitution in this sense is the Constitution of the United States of America. But it is not necessary to look outside the British Commonwealth to find examples of the same sort of thing. Though Britain has no Constitution in this sense, all the other members of the Commonwealth have and so has every colony. There are in all something like seventy separate Constitutions in the Commonwealth and most of them were made in Britain. If printed in full they would occupy many volumes, and if the Constitutions of all the countries of the world were added to them, they would fill many thousands of pages.

This narrower sense of 'constitution' is clearly the most common and it is the sense in which the word will be used in this book. It is worth remembering, however, that there is a connexion between the two uses of the word which can be explained by their history. The wider meaning of 'constitution' is the older meaning. It is the meaning which Bolingbroke intended when he wrote in his essay *On Parties*: 'By Constitution, we mean, whenever we speak with propriety and exactness, that assemblage of laws, institutions and customs, derived from certain fixed principles of reason . . . that compose the general system, according to which the community hath agreed to be governed.' From the earliest times, however, people had thought it proper or necessary to write down in a document the fundamental principles upon which their government for the future should be established and conducted. The Act of Union of the United Provinces of the Netherlands of 1579 is a good example in modern European history. Such a selection or collection of fundamental principles was not usually called 'the Constitution', however, until the time of the American and French Revolutions. The Americans in 1787 declared: 'We, the people of the United States . . . do ordain and establish this Constitution for the United States of America.' Since that time the practice of having a written document containing the principles of governmental organization has become well established and 'Constitution' has come to have this meaning.

It is important to emphasize, however, that although in this book 'Constitution' will be used in its narrower sense, this does not mean that we shall confine ourselves solely to the study of that selection of legal rules to regulate government which is found in a country's Constitution. This selection does not operate in isolation. It is part of the whole system of government or constitutional structure of the country, of the whole collection of rules, legal and non-legal. It is supplemented in particular by legal rules enacted by the legislature, rules which in many countries are almost as important as the rules embodied in the Constitution itself. Thus while a Constitution may establish the principal institutions of government, such as the houses of the legislature, an executive council, and a supreme court, it is often left to the ordinary law to prescribe the composition and mode of appointment of these bodies. Such important branches of constitutional law as the regulation of the electoral system, the distribution of seats, the establishment of government departments, the organization of the judiciary, are in many countries not embodied in the Constitution itself, or, if embodied, are treated only in genera principle; they are dealt with by the ordinary law. In some countries, particularly on the Continent of Europe and in the United States, certain of these laws are described as Organic Laws (*lois organiques*), that is to say, laws which organize institutions, which regulate the exercise of public powers through organs which the Constitution has established. There appears to be a rough division of function between the Constitution which establishes institutions and lays down the broad principles which are to govern them and Organic Laws which regulate their detailed composition and operation. But whether called Organic Laws or not, there is in most countries an important body of legal rules enacted by the legislature which supplements and perhaps modifies or adapts the rules embodied in the Constitution. No Constitution can be properly understood unless its relation to this Organic Law is appreciated.

Legislatures are not the only source of legal rules. Constitutions are supplemented and modified by rules of law which emerge from the interpretations of the Courts. And, outside the realm of legal rules, Constitutions may be supplemented or modified or even nullified by usages, customs, and conventions. These subjects are discussed more fully in Chapters 7 and 8. It is enough to say here that if we are to understand the meaning of a country's Constitution, or to describe its operation or to judge its merit, we must consider it in the wider context of the whole body of constitutional rules of which it is only a part, though often the most important part.

It is perhaps necessary to add what is probably fairly obvious, namely that what a Constitution says is one thing, and what actually happens in practice may be quite another. We must take account of this possible difference in considering the form and worth of Constitutions. What is more, we must be ready to admit that although almost all countries in the world have a Constitution, in many of them the Constitution is treated with neglect or contempt. Indeed in the middle of the twentieth century it can be said that the majority of the world's population lives under systems of government where the government itself and particularly the executive government are of more importance and are treated with more respect or fear than the Constitution. It is only in the states of Western Europe, in the countries of the British Commonwealth, in the United States of America, and in a few Latin-American states that government is carried on with due regard to the limitations imposed by a Constitution; it is only in these states that truly 'constitutional government' can be said to exist. For this reason it is inevitable that in discussing the working of Constitutions in the pages of this book, most attention will be given to these countries, for it is only in them that any considerable material exists for the study of Constitutions. Not that the Constitutions of other countries are completely without interest. On the contrary they embody institutions and theories which are of at least academic interest, while the fact that they are not observed in practice is itself a matter the explanation of which can be most instructive to the student of Constitutions.

Since the Constitution of a country is only a part of that country's whole system of government, does it make any difference whether a country has a Constitution or not? The short answer is that in many countries the fact that there is a Constitution does make a difference. This brings to light a characteristic which most Constitutions exhibit. They are usually endowed with a higher status, in some degree, as a matter of law, than other legal rules in the system of government. At the least it is usually laid down that the amendment of the Constitution can take place only through a special process different from that by which the ordinary law is altered. Sometimes, as in the Constitution of the United States for example, the amendment of the Constitution cannot be undertaken by the legislature alone, but requires the co-operation of other bodies outside. What is more, in the United States, if an act of Congress or an act of any state legislature or of any other rule-making authority in the country, conflicts with the terms of the Constitution, it is void. The same is true in Canada and Australia, in India and Eire, to give a few examples.

There are, however, a few countries where the Constitution may be amended by the legislature by the same process as any ordinary law. New Zealand appears to be an example of this class, at any rate since the passing of the New Zealand Constitution (Amendment) Act of 1947. Is there any substantial difference between this sort of situation and the position which exists in Britain? As a matter of strict law there is no substantial difference. In New Zealand a selection of the more important constitutional rules is embodied in a single document, the Constitution; in the United Kingdom there is no such single document: the rules are scattered about in a number of documents. But in both cases the legislature is supreme over the constitutional rules of law. There are no legal limits on its powers of amendment.

Some people would argue that, strictly speaking, it is not correct to say that a country like New Zealand, whose Constitution can be altered by the ordinary legislative process, really has a Constitution at all. In their view a Constitution must have some degree of supremacy over the legislature; it must be superior to the ordinary law. Where it is found that all the legal rules which purport to govern the government are, in law, on an equal footing with the ordinary law, then a country has no Constitution. This, they argue, is recognized clearly in Britain, more easily perhaps because no one legal document claims the title of 'Constitution'; it should be recognized equally for other countries like New Zealand, even although a particular document is called the 'Constitution'.

It is not necessary to adopt quite so rigid a terminology, provided it is recognized that Constitutions may differ in the extent to which they are superior or supreme in law over the institutions which they create and regulate. This difference is important, but it need not be emphasized to the point of denying the name of 'Constitution' to a document which contains a collection of important rules regulating the government of a country, although those rules do not claim to restrict the powers of the legislature which they may, in fact, have established.

It is natural to ask, in the light of this discussion, why it is that countries have Constitutions, why most of them make the Constitution superior to the ordinary law, and, further, why Britain, at any rate, has no Constitution, in this sense, at all.

If we investigate the origins of modern Constitutions, we find that, practically without exception, they were drawn up and adopted because people wished to make a fresh start, so far as the statement of their system of government was concerned. The desire or need for a fresh start arose either because, as in the United States, some neighbouring communities wished to unite together under a new government; or because, as in Austria or Hungary or Czechoslovakia after 1918, communities had been released from an Empire as the result of a war and were now free to govern themselves; or because, as in France in 1789 or the U.S.S.R. in 1917, a revolution had made a break with the past and a new form of government on new principles was desired; or because, as in Germany after 1918 or in France in 1875 or in 1946, defeat in war had broken the continuity of government and a fresh start was needed after the war. The circumstances in which a break with the past and the need for a fresh start come about vary from country to country, but in almost every case in modern times, countries have a Constitution for the very simple and elementary reason that they wanted, for some reason, to begin again and so they put down in writing the main outline, at least, of their proposed system of government. This has been the practice certainly since 1787 when the American Constitution was drafted, and as the years passed no doubt imitation and the force of example have led all countries to think it necessary to have a Constitution.

This does not explain, however, why many countries think it necessary to give the Constitution a higher status in law than other rules of law. The short explanation of this phenomenon is that in many countries a Constitution is thought of as an instrument by which government can be controlled. Constitutions spring from a belief in limited government. Countries differ however in the extent to which they wish to impose limitations. Sometimes the Constitution limits the executive or subordinate local bodies; sometimes it limits the legislature also, but only so far as amendment of the Constitution itself is concerned; and sometimes it imposes restrictions upon the legislature which go far beyond this point and forbid it to make laws upon certain subjects or in a certain way or with certain effects. Whatever the nature and extent of the restrictions, however, they are based upon a common belief in limited government and in the use of a Constitution to impose these limitations.

The nature of the limitations to be imposed on a government, and therefore the degree to which a Constitution will be supreme over a government, depends upon the objects which the framers of the Constitution wish to safeguard. In the first place they may want to do no more than ensure that the Constitution is not altered casually or carelessly or by subterfuge or implication; they may want to secure that this important document is not lightly tampered with, but solemnly, with due notice and deliberation, consciously amended. In that case it is legitimate to require some special process of constitutional amendment—say that the legislature may amend the Constitution only by a two-thirds majority or after a general election or perhaps upon three months' notice.

The framers of Constitutions often have more than this in mind. They may feel that a certain kind of relationship between the legislature and the executive is important; or that the judicature should have a certain guaranteed degree of independence of the legislature and executive. They may feel that there are certain rights which citizens have and which the legislature or the executive must not invade or remove. They may feel that certain laws should not be made at all. The framers of the American Constitution for example forbade Congress to pass any *ex post facto* law, that is, a law made after the occurrence of the action or situation which it seeks to regulate—a type of law which can render a man guilty of an offence through an action which, when he committed it, was innocent. The framers of the Irish Constitution of 1937 forbade the legislature to pass any law permitting divorce. Further safeguards may be called for when distinct and different communities decide to join together under a common government but are anxious to retain certain rights for themselves. If these communities differ in language, race, and religion, safeguards may be needed to guarantee to them a free exercise of these national characteristics. Those who framed the Swiss, the Canadian, and the South African Constitutions, to name a few only, had to consider these questions. Even when communities do not differ in language, race, or religion, they may still be unwilling to unite unless they are guaranteed a measure of independence inside the union. To meet this demand the Constitution must not only divide powers between the government of the Union and the governments of the individual, component parts, but it must also be supreme in so far at any rate as it enshrines and safeguards this division of powers.

In some countries only one of the considerations mentioned above may operate, in others some, and in some, all. Thus, in the Irish Constitution, the framers were anxious that amendment should be a deliberate process, that the rights of citizens should be safeguarded, and that certain types of laws should not be passed at all, and therefore they made the Constitution supreme and imposed restrictions upon the legislature to achieve these ends. The framers of the American Constitution also had these objects in mind, but on top of that they had to provide for the desire of the thirteen colonies to be united for some purposes only and to remain independent for others. This was an additional reason for giving supremacy to the Constitution and for introducing certain extra safeguards into it.

More will be said about the supremacy of Constitutions and of the special obstacles placed in the way of their amendment in later chapters. Here it is enough to notice that, for a variety of reasons, those who frame Constitutions usually intend them to provide a limitation upon government, though the extent of the limitation varies from case to case.

There are, then, very few Constitutions which do not contain some restriction upon the legislature for some one or more of the reasons mentioned above. Where no restriction is found, the explanation is either that the Constitution is treated with little respect or that, as in New Zealand, it is treated with great respect and that without any legal requirement being inscribed in the Constitution it will be amended only with deliberation and after due consultation with the people.

Why has Britain no Constitution? The question is easier to ask than to answer, and easier to answer at great length—by outlining the constitutional history of Britain—than shortly. But we may suggest a short answer along these lines. Consider the first of the reasons why countries have constitutions—the desire to make a fresh start. Did England ever have this experience? People sometimes speak as if she did not. They talk of an unbroken line of development from earliest times, by which a few rudimentary institutions were adapted and supplemented and finally broadened out and democratized, until absolute monarchy came to be translated into parliamentary democracy. But there *was* a break in English history and when that break came an attempt *was* made to make a fresh start, and to enshrine the new principles of government in a Constitution. The break came with the Civil War in 1642 and the execution of Charles I in 1649. In the years of the Commonwealth and the Protectorate, 1649–1660, several attempts were made to establish a Constitution for the British Isles—not for England alone, for Cromwell had united England, Scotland, and Ireland in one government. The best known of these attempts at a Constitution is the Instrument of Government of 1653. It exhibits all the marks of a Constitution as we understand it today. Had the Commonwealth continued, there is no doubt that there would have been a British Constitution, embodying the fundamental principles of government as they had emerged from the conflicts of the Civil War. Englishmen of that time were ready for a fresh start, they wished to limit government, and they had certain views on the proper relation of executive and legislature and on the rights of the subject. They inscribed these in their various attempts at a Constitution.

In the outcome, however, they could not agree and they could not get enough support for any of their Constitutions. So Charles II returned to the throne and there occurred the Restoration—an important word, for it explains why no Constitution was drawn up in 1660. The return of Charles II looks like a fresh start, but it was not. It meant a return to the old form of government, a restoration of the old system. Those who speak of an unbroken line of development in the history of English government therefore have a good deal of truth on their side. There was a break and an attempt to make a fresh start with a Constitution, but it failed, and the former order was restored.

But, it may be asked, what of the Revolution of 1688 and the Bill of Rights? Was not that a break and a fresh start? Was not the Bill of Rights a Constitution? Here again, England might have had a Constitution but did not. The Bill of Rights certainly deals with constitutional matters. It is concerned particularly with limiting the powers of the King and safeguarding certain rights of the subject. It comes as near to a Constitution as you can get in England. But it covers only a small part of the ground. More important still, it makes no attempt to limit the powers of parliament. Indeed a consequence of the Revolution of 1688 was the development of the complete supremacy or sovereignty of parliament, as a matter of law, in the English system of government.

An interesting and important consequence flows from this. Since parliament becomes the sovereign law-making body, no Constitution could be drawn up to limit the powers of parliament. If limitations were to be placed on the exercise of these legally unrestricted powers, they must be achieved by non-legal means—by public opinion, by elections, by the development of usages and conventions. So it was that, whereas in certain countries of the world in the eighteenth and nineteenth centuries, people were at work framing Constitutions which would limit the powers of legislatures, in Britain parliament was supreme, and it was controlled by political means and not by the law of a Constitution. The British were not less concerned than other people in the assertion of the rights of the subject or in the limitation of governmental activity, but the nature of their constitutional conflicts had resulted in the victory of their parliament over their King; the victory had been complete and parliament stood out as a sovereign body over which no Constitution could be supreme.

We noticed that another reason why countries need a Constitution is that when they unite with others they may wish to preserve certain powers to themselves or to safeguard certain terms in the act of union. Now England united with Scotland in 1707 and with Ireland in 1801, and it is natural to ask why those unions did not produce a Constitution. A first reason is that the unions were not federal unions; they involved in each case the extinction of the local parliament and a full legislative union of Scotland and Ireland with England under one parliament—a parliament which was recognized to be sovereign. No legislative powers, therefore, were to be reserved for Scottish or Irish parliaments, which would need protection in a Constitution. At the same time it is to be noticed that there were certain guarantees given at the time of the union which were regarded as part of the bargain. Thus in the Acts of Union with Scotland and with Ireland certain religious guarantees are recited and it is enacted that they shall remain unaltered for ever. Yet they have been repealed or amended. For the sovereignty of parliament forbids it to bind itself. Once that sovereignty was established no binding Constitution could have been drawn up at the time of the union with Scotland or Ireland which would not have come into conflict with that cardinal principle. No doubt if the English parliament had been willing to permit itself to become controlled by a Constitution at the time of union, it could have been done. But in fact the predominant doctrine of the system of government at that time was the sovereignty of parliament.

It would seem, therefore, that the sort of influences which led other countries to adopt Constitutions either did not apply to England, or operated too late or were overborne by stronger contrary influences. England did make at least one fresh start after a revolutionary break and did attempt to live under a Constitution, but the Restoration put an end to all that. After 1688 the development of the doctrine of the sovereign parliament ruled out any possibility of a Constitution which could control the legislature. The unions with Scotland and Ireland were made within this framework of a sovereign parliament and involved the abolition of their own parliaments. So at every stage when Britain might have had a Constitution, it was prevented.

This is not to say that Britain could not have a Constitution. It may come about that public opinion strongly demands that the powers of parliament be legally limited by a Constitution as those of the parliament of Eire are, and this opinion might prevail. If a federal system came to be established in Britain, a supreme Constitution would have to be drawn up. All that can be said so far is that this has not yet happened and that if it is to be done the law of the British system of government would have to be changed—the doctrine of the sovereignty of parliament would have to be abolished. Britain could have a Constitution, however, without going as far as this. There is no reason why the principal legal rules that govern the government should not be collected into one consolidated measure and be enacted by parliament. This Constitution would have no superior status to any other act of parliament; it would not be binding upon parliament, but it would of course be binding upon every other institution and person in the land. It would have the same sort of position in the law of the land as the Constitution of New Zealand has in that country. It would be an interesting and perhaps revealing document; it would certainly contain some of the greatest statements in constitutional history. Yet most Englishmen would regard its compilation and enactment as, if not a waste of time, an academic exercise—which is, they might feel, almost the same thing. After all, as Mr. Podsnap said to the French gentleman in *Our Mutual Friend*:

'We Englishmen are very proud of our Constitution, sir. It was bestowed upon us by Providence. No other country is so favoured as this country.' . . .

'And *other* countries,' said the foreign gentleman. 'They do how?'

'They do, sir,' returned Mr. Podsnap, gravely shaking his head; 'they do —I am sorry to be obliged to say it—*as* they do.'

'It was a little particular of Providence,' said the foreign gentleman, laughing, 'for the frontier is not large.'

'Undoubtedly,' assented Mr. Podsnap; 'But so it is. It was the Charter of the Land. This Island was blest, sir, to the direct exclusion of such other countries as—as there may happen to be. And if we were all Englishmen present, I would say . . . that there is in the Englishman a combination of qualities, a modesty, an independence, a responsibility, a repose, combined with an absence of everything calculated to call a blush into the cheek of a young person, which one would seek in vain among the Nations of the Earth.'

Such a people, it will be readily admitted, has no need of a Constitution. But, as Mr. Podsnap indicated, other countries do as they do, and this being so, it is necessary for us to turn now and see how they do.

2
How Constitutions may be Classified

IT USED TO BE the fashion to classify Constitutions into written
Constitutions and unwritten Constitutions, and also to offer Britain
as the sole surviving example of this latter class. It will be apparent
that the definition of 'Constitution' adopted in this book implies that
virtually all Constitutions are written. We have chosen to regard the
word 'Constitution' as describing a selection of the more important
legal rules which govern a government, embodied in a document
or sometimes, as in Sweden perhaps, in a collection of documents.
Most countries of the world have a written Constitution in this sense.
The truth about Britain can be stated not by saying that she has an
unwritten Constitution but by saying rather that she has no written
Constitution.

But people who spoke of the distinction between written and unwritten Constitutions had an important distinction in mind. They
were thinking of the distinction between those rules regulating a
government—mostly rules of law—which are written down either
in a Constitution or in some act of parliament or other legal
document, and those other rules, mainly the customs and conventions and usages regulating the government, which have usually
not been precisely formulated and put in writing. There was perhaps a certain rough accuracy in describing this distinction as a
distinction between written and unwritten rules in a system of
government, though even this may be doubted. Some rules of law
are unwritten, in the sense that they are not inscribed in a Constitution or in statutes; some conventions have been put down in
writing. In the preamble to the Statute of Westminster, 1931, there

is an example of a constitutional convention which binds the parliament of the United Kingdom and of the Dominions in the following terms: 'It would be in accord with the established constitutional position of all the members of the Commonwealth in relation to one another that any alteration in the law touching the Succession to the Throne or the Royal Style and Titles shall hereafter require the assent as well of the Parliaments of all the Dominions as of the Parliament of the United Kingdom.'

But even if we overlook the exceptions to the general equation of rules of law and non-legal rules with written and unwritten rules respectively, we cannot agree that there is any country, least of all the United Kingdom, which has a system of government embodied solely in written rules or solely in unwritten rules. In the last chapter it was stressed that in all countries and not least in Britain both legal and non-legal rules, written and unwritten, are blended together to form the system of government. Whether we use the term 'Constitution' narrowly—as we have chosen to do in this book—or widely, to include the whole system of government, Britain has not got an unwritten Constitution and it would be hard to think of any country which has. The classification of Constitutions into written and unwritten should therefore be discarded. The better distinction is that between countries which have a written Constitution and those which have no written Constitution, or, more simply, and following the definition of Constitution adopted in this book, between countries which have a Constitution and those which have not. At the same time the distinction between rules of law and non-legal rules within the whole body of rules which regulate a government is certainly valuable and important. In a later chapter the interaction of these two classes of rule upon each other will be discussed, with particular reference to the effect of usages and conventions upon the law of a Constitution.

Constitutions may be classified according to the method by which they may be amended. We may place in one category those Constitutions which may be amended by the legislature through the same process as any other law, and we may place in another category those Constitutions which require a special process for their amendment. The first class is very small. The Constitution of New Zealand is one of the few examples which can be cited. In the other class lie most of the Constitutions of the world, varying from those like that of the U.S.S.R., which merely requires a two-thirds majority in each house of the Supreme Soviet, to those of the United States, Switzerland, or Australia, where the parliament itself alone cannot amend the Constitution but requires the co-operation and consent of other bodies or of the people. This method of classifying Constitutions has usually been described as a classification into flexible and rigid Constitutions, a classification which owes its origin to Lord Bryce and is expounded by him in his *Studies in History and Jurisprudence*. Where no special process is required to amend a Constitution, it is called 'flexible'; where a special process is required, a Constitution is called 'rigid'.

This form of classification has some value. It is based upon a real and valid distinction. The terms 'flexible' and 'rigid' have the advantage that they can be used to indicate differences of degree. We can say that, since the legal obstacles to amendment of the Constitution in the United States, Australia, Denmark, and Switzerland are so much greater than they are, for example, in Norway, France, or the U.S.S.R., then the Constitutions of the first four countries are more rigid than those of the latter three. It is possible to arrange Constitutions according to the degree of rigidity, though no doubt it would be difficult in some cases to decide which of two sets of obstacles to amendment created the greater degree of rigidity. Such comparisons, however, probably provide instructive study.

The classification of Constitutions into 'rigid' and 'flexible', in the sense in which these terms have been explained above, however, has certain disadvantages. To begin with, although it tells us something about Constitutions it does not tell us much. A system of classification which places almost all the Constitutions of the world in one category of 'rigid' and leaves only one or two in the other cannot take us very far. What is more, the terms themselves tend inevitably to mislead. They lead us to think that a Constitution which contains a number of legal obstacles to its amendment will be harder to alter and will therefore be less frequently altered than one which contains fewer obstacles or no special obstacles at all. Now it is true that this is a misinterpretation of what the distinction of 'rigid' and 'flexible' was intended to mean. It referred only to certain formal requirements in the legal process of amendment. Inevitably, however, the terms come to be used more loosely, so that a rigid Constitution is thought of as a Constitution which, because it contains legal obstacles, is hard to alter and is seldom altered; a flexible Constitution is thought of as a Constitution which, because no special process is required for its amendment, is easy to alter and is often altered. In fact this unwarranted conclusion is not borne out by the facts. The Swiss Constitution which is 'rigid', in terms of its legal amending process, has been altered more often and more easily than, say, the Constitution of the Third Republic in France, the amendment of which required no more than a joint meeting of the two houses, the Chamber of Deputies and the Senate. The Australian Constitution, on the other hand, which has substantially the same amending process as the Swiss, has been amended four times only in twenty-three attempts.

The fact is that the ease or the frequency with which a Constitution is amended depends not only on the legal provisions which prescribe the method of change but also on the predominant political and social groups in the community and the extent to which they are satisfied with or acquiesce in the organization and distribution of political power which the Constitution prescribes. If the Constitution suits them, they will not alter it much, even if the alteration requires no more than an ordinary act of parliament. Against their opposition, too, attempts at amendment by dissatisfied minorities cannot hope to succeed. If, on the other hand, enough of them wish to see the Constitution altered, it will be done, even if the process involves the surmounting of special legal obstacles. This is not to say that these legal obstacles are unimportant. A minority of the electors can prevent a constitutional change in Australia, Switzerland, Denmark, and the United States. But these legal obstacles are part, not the whole, of the circumstances which will determine whether a Constitution is going to be easily and frequently changed or not.

In the light of these considerations it may be wiser, perhaps, to use the terms 'flexible' and 'rigid' to distinguish Constitutions not according to whether or not they require for their amendment a special procedure which is not required for ordinary laws, but according to whether they are in practice, through the force of a variety of circumstances, easily and often altered or not. This would be a departure from the original meaning of the terms as Bryce first used them, but it would be less misleading. On this distinction the Constitutions of Australia, Denmark, Norway, the United States, and France under the Third Republic, would perhaps be among the examples of rigid Constitutions; those of Switzerland and South Africa would be examples of flexible Constitutions.

There is another method of classifying Constitutions which has a close relation to that of 'rigid' and 'flexible' as originally defined. Constitutions are divided into a category of those which are supreme over the legislature—that is to say, which cannot be amended by the legislature—and those which are not. This classification involves a sub-division of the category of 'rigid'. You take those Constitutions whose amendment requires a special process and you put on one side those in which the process is not within the sole competence of the legislature. These Constitutions are supreme over the legisla-ture. Some examples of supreme Constitutions, in this sense, are those of the United States, Australia, Switzerland, Eire, and Denmark.

It is not always easy however to say whether a Constitution is supreme or not. Take the case of Belgium. When the Belgian parliament proposes an alteration in the Constitution, a dissolution of both Houses follows. After the general election, the amendment is carried if at least two thirds of the members of each House are present and if at least two thirds of those present vote in favour of the proposed amendment. Clearly the actual amendment is made by the legislature. To that extent the legislature is supreme over the Constitution. But the requirement of a general election between the two votes comes near to a requirement that the amendment must be submitted to the electors for approval, and suggests that, in practice, the electorate and not the legislature is supreme over the Constitution. The concurrence of the people is required for any change. On this argument it would seem that Belgium should be placed along with the United States, Australia, Switzerland, Eire, and Denmark in the class of countries which have a supreme Con-stitution. For substantially similar reasons Holland, Sweden, and Norway would be in the same category.

But what is to be said of a country like the U.S.S.R. or South Africa or Finland which provides that amendments to the Con-stitution, in whole or in part, may be made by the legislature but only if a special majority is obtained? Here clearly the legislature makes the amendment and is not required by the Constitution to give any other body an opportunity to express an opinion. Is it not supreme over the Constitution? The answer would seem to be that if the legislature is bound to follow the procedure laid down in the Constitution and to observe the requirements concerning majorities there inserted, the legislature is to that extent controlled by the Constitution and the Constitution is to that extent supreme over the legislature. Authorities differ in their attitude to requirements of this kind. There was a substantial body of expert opinion in South Africa, for example, which held that, in strict law, the legislature of the Union was not bound by the requirements about special majorities in the Constitution. This view was rejected by the Supreme Court of South Africa in 1952 in the case of *Harris* v. *Dönges* when it was held that the requirements must be adhered to. However, it will be appreciated that the supremacy or controlling power of the Constitution in such a situation may not amount to much.

Constitutions may be classified also in terms of the method by which the powers of government are distributed between the government of the whole country and any local governments which exercise authority over parts of the country. On this principle Constitutions are classified as 'federal' or 'unitary'. In a federal Constitution the powers of government are divided between a government for the whole country and governments for parts of the country in such a way that each government is legally independent within its own sphere. The government for the whole country has its own area of powers and it exercises them without any control from the governments of the constituent parts of the country, and these latter in their turn exercise their powers without being controlled by the central government. In particular the legislature of the whole country has limited powers, and the legislatures of the states or provinces have limited powers. Neither is subordinate to the other; both are co-ordinate. In a unitary Constitution, on the other hand, the legislature of the whole country is the supreme law-making body in the country. It may permit other legislatures to exist and to exercise their powers, but it has the right, in law, to overrule them; they are subordinate to it.

Among examples of a federal Constitution there may be mentioned those of the United States, Switzerland, and Australia. In each case the Constitution sets out the matters upon which the legislature of the whole country may make laws, and it reserves to the states or cantons a sphere in which their legislatures may operate in legal independence of the central legislature and of each other. The Constitution of Canada is more difficult to classify. It establishes an independent government for the whole country, but it permits that government to exercise certain limited powers of control over the governments of the ten provinces. Although there is a list of subjects enumerated in the Constitution over which the provincial legislatures have exclusive authority and upon which the parliament of Canada is unable to legislate, yet it is provided that the executive government of Canada may veto provincial bills or disallow provincial acts—and this power has been exercised from time to time. Moreover provincial judges are appointed by the government of Canada, and the formal head of the provincial government—the Lieutenant-Governor—is also appointed by the government of Canada. These qualifications upon the strict federal principle of independent and co-ordinate status between general and provincial governments may lead us to regard the Canadian Constitution as not strictly federal. It may be called quasi-federal.

Yet here again it is interesting to compare the law of the Constitution with the practice of government. Although the powers of veto and disallowance have been exercised by the government of Canada over provincial legislation, they have been used sparingly and they have done little to contradict in practice the independent status of the provinces. In Australia on the other hand, where the law of the Constitution safeguards the independence of the states more strictly, the control of the government of the Commonwealth of Australia over the governments of the states has become so great that some observers would say that in practice the states of Australia are little more than the administrative agencies of the Commonwealth. This control has come chiefly from the greater financial resources of the Commonwealth and has shown itself particularly in the increased reliance of the states upon grants from the Commonwealth for the performance of most of their important functions. It might be said therefore that the Australian Constitution works in practice like a unitary Constitution embodying a considerable measure of decentralization or devolution, although in law it remains federal. In Canada on the other hand the Constitution, though in law quasi-federal, is in practice nearer to federalism than the Australian.

In the class of quasi-federal Constitutions it is probably proper to include the Indian Constitution of 1950; the Constitution of the West German Republic of 1949 and also that of the German ('Weimar') Republic from 1918 to 1933; and the Constitution of the U.S.S.R. of 1936.

The class of unitary Constitutions is large—so large indeed that one may wonder whether for purposes of classification it is of value. It includes countries like New Zealand or France or Sweden, Norway, and Denmark, whose only authorities subordinate to the central legislature are local government bodies with fairly closely controlled powers. It includes also countries like South Africa, where there are established, under the parliament of the Union, separate councils for each of the provinces of the Union, with powers to make ordinances upon a list of subjects enumerated in the Constitution. Here is a wide degree of decentralization or 'devolution' as it is sometimes called. It is possible, too, that the Constitution of the U.S.S.R., in spite of the fact that it describes itself as federal and might be classified in law as quasi-federal, should be placed in practice in the class of unitary constitutions with a wide measure of decentralization. Quite apart from practice, however, the extent of the powers conferred upon the central government of the U.S.S.R. by the Constitution of 1936 is so very large, and the degree of control, particularly of financial control, over the constituent republics permitted by the Constitution to the central government is so far-reaching, that the federal element, even in the law of the Constitution, is insignificant.

While the distinction between 'federal' and 'unitary' Constitutions has some value therefore, in that it enables us to segregate federal Constitutions from the rest, its value is limited. The class of unitary Constitutions is so wide and varied, the degree and method of decentralization in practice in unitary Constitutions is so diverse, that a good deal more must be known about a Constitution described as 'unitary' before we can feel that we know what it is like.

Moreover it is always necessary in dealing with Constitutions which in the letter of the law are federal or unitary, to discover how in practice the law operates. A Constitution, unitary and highly centralized on paper, may be almost federal in practice; a federal Constitution may be, in practice, unitary, as indeed are the so-called federal Constitutions of Mexico, Venezuela, Brazil, and the Argentine.

It must follow that Constitutions which are federal are also supreme and, in the original sense of the term as Bryce used it, 'rigid'. In a federal Constitution the legislatures both of the whole country and of its parts are limited in their powers and independent of each other. Consequently they must not be able, acting alone, to alter the Constitution so far at any rate as the distribution of powers between them is concerned. They are not subordinate to each other but they must all be subordinate to the Constitution. If the Congress of the United States, for example, could alter the Constitution as it chose, it could increase its powers at the expense of the states. To that extent the states would be subordinate to the Congress and the Constitution would be unitary, not federal. So also the Congress must not be subordinate to the states. The supremacy of the Constitution over all the legislatures of the country, and the rigidity of the Constitution, are essential characteristics of a federal Constitution and they flow necessarily from the idea of federalism itself.

It is sometimes imagined that while a Constitution, if it is federal, must be supreme and rigid, a Constitution which is unitary will not be supreme or rigid. Enough has been said already perhaps to show that this is not necessarily so. To say that a Constitution is supreme is to describe its relation to the legislature of the country and to declare that the legislature's power to alter the Constitution is either limited or non-existent. To say that a Constitution is unitary is to make an assertion not about the relationship of the legislature to the Constitution but of the legislature to other law-making bodies in the country, an assertion that the legislature of the whole country is superior to any other such law-making body.

An example will illustrate the point. New Zealand and the Irish Republic are both unitary states; in each case the parliament of the country is supreme over other law-making bodies inside the country. But the Constitution of New Zealand is not supreme and it is not rigid; the parliament of New Zealand may amend it at any time by the ordinary process of legislation. The Constitution of the Irish Republic, however, is supreme and rigid. It limits the power of the legislature in law-making, for example by prohibiting the making of laws permitting divorce, and it can be altered only by a special process which involves a referendum to the people. Indeed the Constitutions of most unitary states are supreme and rigid and in this respect unitary states do not differ from federal states. Most countries at present have chosen to have supreme and rigid Constitutions.

Before we leave our discussion of the distinction between federal and unitary Constitutions, it is well to mention a further class of Constitution which is linked with these two. It was said that, if in a country the government of the whole country and the governments of the constituent parts were not subordinate one to another but rather co-ordinate with each other, then that country had a federal Constitution, whereas if the governments of the constituent parts of a country were subordinate to the government of the whole, then the country had a unitary Constitution. But there remains a third possibility. Supposing the government of the whole country is subordinate to the governments of the parts, what form of Constitution is thereby set up? It is usual to call such a Constitution a 'confederation' or a confederate Constitution. These are not very convenient terms. They are often used as equivalent to the words 'federation' and 'federal'. Thus the Swiss Constitution, which is federal, describes itself officially as 'Constitution fédérale de la Confédération suisse'; while in Canada where, as we have seen, the Constitution has leanings towards the unitary form of government, it is customary to speak of the union of the provinces as 'confederation'.

In spite of these difficulties the word 'confederation' may be used to describe a form of association between governments whereby they set up a common organization to regulate matters of common concern but retain to themselves, to a greater or less degree, some control over this common organization. It is often doubtful whether the common organization can be said to possess sufficient power to be called a government, and in that case it may be doubtful sometimes whether the document which establishes this common organization should be called a 'Constitution'—it might more properly be called an agreement, a covenant, or a treaty.

There have been a number of examples in the past of confederate Constitutions. Before the present federal Constitution of the United States came into operation in 1789 the States regulated their common affairs through the Articles of Confederation, a leading characteristic of which was (to quote a contemporary writer, Alexander Hamilton in *The Federalist*) that 'the concurrence of thirteen distinct sovereign wills is requisite, under the Confederation, to the complete execution of every important measure that proceeds from the union'. The United Netherlands were governed by a confederate Constitution from 1579; the various German Constitutions—that from 1815 to 1867, the North German Confederation of 1867–71, and the Constitution of the German Empire from 1871 to 1918—were all, in varying degrees, confederate; and the Austro-Hungarian Compromise, which lasted from 1867 to 1918, also embodied the principle of confederation. In later times the Statute of the Council of Europe might be thought to provide an example of a confederate Constitution, but it is doubtful whether it can be said to grant sufficient powers to the common organization to justify the use of the word 'Constitution'. It would fall more appropriately into the class in which we find the Covenant of the League of Nations and the Charter of the United Nations Organization, which rightly are not called Constitutions because they do not establish a common government for their constituent members, but rather a common organization.

The classification of Constitutions into federal, unitary, and confederate is based upon the principle by which the powers of government are distributed in the Constitution between the government for the whole country and any governments which may be established for its constituent parts. But it is possible to classify Constitutions also in terms of the method by which powers are distributed inside a government between the various organs or institutions which make up that government, whether it be a government for the whole of a country or the government of a part only. On this principle Constitutions have been classified into those which embody, to a greater or less degree, the doctrine of the separation of powers, and those which do not; or, what is often regarded as substantially the same thing, those which establish the presidential executive and those which provide for the parliamentary executive. It is necessary to say a word or two to elucidate these distinctions.

Stated in its simplest and most extreme form the doctrine of the separation of powers means that each of the processes of government —let us say they are legislative, executive or administrative, and judicial—is confided exclusively to a separate institution of government. There must be no overlapping either of functions or of persons. In this extreme form the separation of powers has seldom, if ever, existed. But it is possible to find some Constitutions where it is an important or even a predominant feature of the system of government, and others again where its contradiction is equally an important or predominant feature. The Constitution of the United States is usually quoted as the leading example of a Constitution embodying the doctrine of the separation of powers. Indeed it goes a long way in this direction. It is clearly stated in the Constitution that 'all legislative powers herein granted shall be vested in a Congress of the United States', that 'the executive power shall be vested in a President of the United States of America', and that 'the judicial power of the United States shall be vested in one Supreme Court and in such inferior courts as the Congress may from time to time ordain and establish'. Thus the processes of government are confided exclusively, it would seem, to three institutions. Moreover the Constitution takes care to separate these institutions from each other. The President may not sit in Congress nor may any other person do so while holding an office under the United States. There can be no overlapping of persons between the three institutions.

This distinction of the three processes of government in the American Constitution, and their allocation to separate institutions, is the basis upon which that Constitution has been classified as one embodying the separation of powers. Moreover as the separation of the institutions means that the head of the executive, the President, and his subordinates cannot sit in Congress, the Constitution is often described as establishing the presidential or non-parliamentary executive.

These conclusions are substantially true, but they should be qualified in one respect. The American Constitution separates the three institutions—Congress, the President (with his officers), and

B

the Judiciary—and forbids overlapping of personnel between them, but it does not distribute each of the three processes to one of these institutions with absolute exclusiveness. In spite of the very definite words which have been quoted, the Constitution does introduce some qualifications. Thus, although all legislative powers are granted to Congress, the President has power to veto its acts and his veto can be overridden only by a two-thirds majority in both houses; although executive power is vested in the President, he must ask the advice and consent of the Senate for the making of treaties and for important appointments, including those of members of his own cabinet; and although judicial power is vested in a supreme court and subordinate courts, the Senate is empowered to try impeachments, including an impeachment on the President, although when a trial of the President on impeachment occurs, the Chief Justice of the United States presides over the Senate. These few examples are enough to show that there is not a complete separation of the processes of government in the United States; they overlap from one of the carefully separated institutions to another. The institutions themselves, however, are much more rigidly separated, and it is this aspect of the separation of powers which distinguishes the American Constitution more obviously from some others.

This difference may be illustrated at once if we look at, say, the Irish Constitution, the Indian Constitution, or the South African or Australian Constitutions, where it is laid down that the ministers, the heads of the executive, must be members of the parliament. These Constitutions establish, that is to say, a parliamentary executive—the form of government, often called 'cabinet government', with which we are familiar in Britain, in the other members of the British Commonwealth, and in the countries of Western Europe. It should be emphasized, however, that while the presidential or non-parliamentary executive, where it exists, is usually enshrined in the Constitution, the system of the parliamentary executive is not always described or laid down in the actual Constitution but rests upon other rules of law and even more upon usage and convention.

It is necessary to stress also that a separation of the processes of government need not be confined to cases where there is a presidential executive. It would be quite possible for a Constitution to provide that legislative powers are to be vested in a parliament and must not be delegated to any other institution, and to provide at the same time that ministers must be members of parliament. Indeed the Constitution of the Fourth French Republic, which envisaged a parliamentary executive, though it did not explicitly prescribe it, declared, in Article 13, that 'the National Assembly alone shall vote the laws. It may not delegate this right.' A linking of institutions is not inconsistent with a separation of processes. It is true that such cases are rare, but it is important to recognize the distinction.

It may be noted also that even in countries where the doctrine of the separation of powers appears to be rejected—where legislative powers may be exercised by the executive without restriction, and where the heads of the executive sit in parliament—it is usually applied to a large extent where the judicial process is concerned. Indeed in almost all countries where the Constitution establishes or permits the parliamentary executive, and the linking or fusing of functions and institutions, it establishes also the independence or separation of the judiciary to a substantial degree. It is true that in many of those countries judicial functions are sometimes confided to the executive; that the appointment of judges is in the hands of the executive; and that the judges may be removed on an address by both houses of the legislature. But the independence of the judiciary and its separate existence are recognized none the less as strongly in such countries as is the organic connexion of the executive and the legislature.

In distinguishing Constitutions which provide for the presidential or non-parliamentary executive from those which prescribe the parliamentary executive it is important not to state the difference in too extreme a form. The distinction does not mean that whereas in the United States the President and his subordinates may not sit in Congress, in a country with the parliamentary executive the Prime Minister and all the other members of the executive may sit in parliament. Not at all. In a country with a parliamentary executive, the great majority of the members of the executive—the civil servants or office holders—are excluded from parliament. It is only the heads of the departments, the ministers, who must or may sit in parliament. There is, indeed, under the system of the parliamentary executive just as rigid a separation of institutions as under the presidential executive from the bottom upwards, but when you reach the top of the scale the difference is found. This difference is a very important difference, but its nature must be clearly understood. The principle enshrined in the rule of the American Constitution that 'no person holding any office under the United States shall be a Member of either House during his continuance in office' is part of the law in all countries with a parliamentary executive, subject to exceptions being made in the case of ministers. These exceptions make all the difference. But they are exceptions.

Most systems of government fall into one or other of the categories of the parliamentary or the non-parliamentary executive. As a rule a country which has a non-parliamentary executive will have that form of government embodied explicitly in its Constitution. Where the parliamentary executive prevails, it may be either embodied in the Constitution to a greater or less extent, as in Ireland, India, Australia, and South Africa, or assumed and permitted and largely regulated by custom and by ordinary law, as in New Zealand or Canada, Holland, and Belgium, or the Scandinavian monarchies. There are examples in between, such as France, where, in the Constitution of the Fifth Republic, though it is provided that ministers are to be responsible to the National Assembly and may be dismissed by it, there is an explicit requirement that neither the Prime Minister nor any other member of the government may be a member of either house of parliament—a curious hybrid of the two systems, the success of which remains to be seen.

The presidential or non-parliamentary executive is found chiefly in countries whose Constitutions have been based upon or greatly influenced by the Constitution of the United States. It prevails in all the countries of North, South, and Central America, with the exception of Canada. It is found also in the Philippine Republic and in Liberia.

An important example of a Constitution which does not fall exactly into one or other of these two classes is the Swiss. The executive in Switzerland—the Federal Council—is elected by the two houses of the parliament sitting jointly after a general election, and its composition reflects the state of parties in the parliament. Its members hold office for a fixed term of four years—the period of life of the lower house of the parliament. But they may not while holding office as Federal Councillors be members of the parliament, though they are entitled to sit and speak in either house. To the extent that the Federal Council has a fixed term of office, irrespective of changes of opinion in the parliament, and inasmuch as its members may not be members of the parliament, the Swiss executive resembles the presidential or non-parliamentary executive. But since it is chosen by the parliament on party lines, after a general election, and since its members normally speak and sit in the parliament, it has a resemblance also to the parliamentary executive. It is an interesting and successful combination of two systems.

It is necessary to notice in conclusion a method of classifying Constitutions which was once considered to be of prime importance, namely a classification into republican and monarchical Constitutions. Nowadays this distinction has less significance. It means little more than that where the head of a state is a president, then that state is a republic, and where the head of the state is a king, that state is a monarchy or kingdom. But as in fact the status and powers of a president differ so much in republican constitutions, and the powers of kings in monarchies also, this classification groups together states so different that it is difficult to find more than a small nominal similarity between them. Thus in the category of republics are included the United States, the U.S.S.R., Switzerland, France, Portugal, all the Central and South American states, Finland, India, and the Republic of Ireland. In the United States the president is not only the head of the state, he is the head of the government also; but his powers are limited by the Constitution. In the Constitutions of Central and South America a similar position is accorded to the president in law, but in practice in many cases he exercises power with little or no regard to the Constitution. In the U.S.S.R., France, India, Ireland, Portugal, and Switzerland, the president is head of the state but not head of the government, yet in each case there are important differences in his position.

When we consider modern monarchies, such as those of the United Kingdom and other members of the British Commonwealth, or of the Scandinavian countries or of Holland and Belgium, we find a greater similarity between the position of the king in such countries and the president in, say, the republics of India, Ireland, Switzerland, and even the U.S.S.R., than there is between the president in these republics and the president in the American republics.

Nowadays a classification of Constitutions into republican and monarchical produces so heterogeneous a grouping that it illustrates differences rather than similarities between Constitutions. Its chief value lies in its illustration of the fact that the symbols of monarchy are not incompatible with free government and that the symbols of a republic may not prevent autocracy.

The distinction between a republican and a monarchical Constitution once had considerable meaning and importance. It stood for the difference between what may be called popular or democratic government and absolutism, autocracy, or dictatorship. A monarch, as the name implies, was a sole ruler; he was responsible to himself alone. It is difficult today to find examples of this 'absolute monarchy' as it is usually called—certainly the monarchs of Ethiopia or Persia can hardly be regarded as absolute, sole rulers. The transformation of absolute monarchies into constitutional or limited monarchies has brought about the position that wherever monarchies exist today—with a few possible exceptions—the Constitution provides for democratic or popular government. Modern monarchies have come to resemble closely what a republic was intended to be; republican Constitutions on the other hand illustrate almost every system of government from democracy to dictatorship.

It would be an error to suppose, however, that a modern constitutional monarchy is no more than 'a crowned republic'. The kingship in the countries of the British Commonwealth or in the Scandinavian states or in the Low Countries is an institution with a symbolism, a political and social significance, and a national character which no presidency possesses. The virtues which monarchy exhibits, no less than the dangers to which it is prone, mark it off as a distinct form not of Constitution and government only but also of society and community. These things are not easily stated but they exist and their recognition and apprehension is necessary if the classification of Constitutions into monarchies and republics is to be rightly appreciated.

It will have been seen that few of the methods by which Constitutions may be classified expose differences that are significant, and it may be wondered whether it is really worth while to attempt such classifications. It must be conceded at once that classification of

Constitutions has but a limited value, if only because a Constitution itself, as we have emphasized, is only a part of the rules that make up a system of government, and any category into which a Constitution may be placed may be rendered unreal or inadequate by the study of the actual working of the system of government. On the other hand there is some value, if indeed but a limited value, to be obtained from an attempt to classify Constitutions, more particularly when a Constitution is considered in relation to all the possible methods of classification. We discover something of value, for example, when we are able to say that the Constitution of the United States is written, that it is rigid, that it is supreme, that it is federal, that it establishes a presidential or non-parliamentary executive, and that it is republican. We assert something of significance also when we say that while the Australian Constitution resembles the American in that both are written, rigid, supreme, and federal, the Australian, unlike the American, establishes a parliamentary executive and is monarchical, not republican. We assert something significant also when we say that while the Constitutions of Eire and New Zealand resemble each other in that both are written and unitary and both establish a parliamentary executive, they differ in that the Irish Constitution is rigid and supreme, while the Constitution of New Zealand is flexible and subordinate to the legislature, and in that the Irish Constitution is republican and that of New Zealand is monarchical. And finally, even if the result of the attempt to classify a Constitution should reveal the inadequacy and unreality of the various bases of classification so far as that particular Constitution is concerned, the process by which we arrive at this result usually teaches us a lot about the significance of the Constitution, of its place in the system of government of which it is a part, and of what is living and what is dead in the collection of rules, legal and non-legal, which governs a government in any country.

What a Constitution should Contain

A GLANCE at the Constitutions of different countries shows at once that people differ very much in what they think it necessary for a Constitution to contain. The Norwegians were able to say all that they wanted to say in about twenty-five pages; the Indians occupy about two hundred and fifty pages in their Constitution of 1950. A principal line of division is found between those who regard a Constitution as primarily and almost exclusively a legal document in which, therefore, there is a place for rules of law but for practically nothing else, and those who think of a Constitution as a sort of manifesto, a confession of faith, a statement of ideals, a 'charter of the land', as Mr Podsnap called it.

Constitutions drafted in Britain or under the influence of British legal doctrines almost always fall into the first class. They may contain a few flourishes in the preamble, but for the most part they confine themselves to rules of law. Rather less austere are the Constitutions of Holland and Belgium and the Scandinavian countries; the Constitution of the United States similarly permits itself occasional excursions into political theory. Most other Constitutions, however—and these include the Constitutions of some of the member states in the American Union—contain material which is either not strictly constitutional by nature or, if it is constitutional, is not really law or susceptible of expression in rules of law. An example of the inclusion within a Constitution of matter which is not constitutional by nature is the provision, inserted in the Swiss Constitution (*Article 25 bis*) in 1893, which prohibits the sticking of animals for butchers' meat unless they have previously been stunned. On the other hand many modern Constitutions contain declarations of the rights of the subject, or of political objectives, or of the source and ends of government which, while more or less relevant to the study of constitutional questions, are not reduced and are often incapable of being reduced to rules of law.

It is not easy to get agreement among those responsible for drafting Constitutions upon what is the best practice to adopt. When the South African Constitution was drawn up in 1909, the draftsman, in his prosaic way, thought that the best opening section would be: 'This Act may be cited as the South Africa Act, 1909'—admittedly short and to the point, a section necessary somewhere in the Act, and, in its way, informative. But some South Africans were very unhappy about this way of opening their Constitution, and they worked valiantly for its amendment. They were successful in 1925. The offending section was removed to the very end of the Constitution, and in its place were substituted these words: 'The people of the Union acknowledge the sovereignty and guidance of Almighty God.' This, needless to say, is not a rule of law and is only remotely constitutional, but it expressed a sentiment which some South Africans wished to place on record at the outset of the statement of their system of government.

Where opinions differ so much, it may seem presumptuous for an academic student to express an opinion, more particularly when his opinion will be in opposition to the practice adopted by the majority of modern Constitution makers. Yet the great authority of John Marshall, Chief Justice of the United States from 1801 to 1835 and himself a principal architect of the American Constitution, may be invoked in support of the opinion which is to be advanced in this chapter. 'A Constitution,' said Marshall in 1819, in the case of *McCulloch* v. *Maryland* (4 Wheaton 316), 'to contain an accurate detail of all the subdivisions of which its great powers will admit, and of all the means by which they may be carried into execution, would partake of the prolixity of a legal code, and could scarcely be embraced by the human mind. It would probably never be understood by the public. Its nature, therefore, requires that only its great outlines should be marked, its important objects designated, and the minor ingredients which compose those objects be deduced from the nature of the objects themselves.' To the question: 'What should a Constitution contain?' the short answer, then, is: 'The very minimum, and that minimum to be rules of law.' One essential characteristic of the ideally best form of Constitution is that it should be as short as possible.

To say this, however, does not take us very far. Such an answer avoids the difficulties which confront all Constitution makers when they come to ask just what it is possible to leave out, if they are to frame a Constitution which will prove acceptable to those who are to operate it or live under it. It is necessary therefore to look rather carefully at the problems which have confronted Constitution makers in a country before we can decide what is the irreducible minimum which it would have sufficed to enshrine in the Constitution. That is not to say that it is impossible to conceive an ideally best form of Constitution. It is true that there is no one form of Constitution which is practicable or suitable or eligible for all communities. But it is possible to conceive a form of Constitution which, if adopted by those communities for which it is practicable and suitable and eligible, would be attended with the greatest amount of beneficial consequences, immediate and prospective. Some hints about the characteristics of an ideally best form of Constitution will emerge when we consider what communities have inserted into their Constitutions and ask how much of this is really necessary and unavoidable, and of this irreducible minimum, how much is to be regretted or deplored.

It would seem at first sight that a community which was content to adopt a unitary form of government would be able, other things being equal, to frame a simpler and shorter Constitution than a community or a collection of communities which wished to adopt a federal form of government. For in a unitary government, one would suppose, the Constitution needs to provide no more than the structure, in general terms, of the legislature, the executive, and the judiciary; the nature in broad outline of their mutual relations; and the nature of their relations to the community itself. The detailed working out of these principles and the adaptation of the Constitution to changing needs and times can be left to the legislature to regulate itself. For a federal government, however, it is necessary that the Constitution should mark out the spheres in which the government of the whole country and the governments of the constituent parts should have authority; it must place limitations upon all the legislatures; and it must secure the supremacy of the Constitution itself over the legislatures, ensuring, incidentally, that, by whatever means the Constitution may be amended, it should not be made subordinate, so far at least as the division of powers is concerned, either to the legislature of the whole country or to the legislatures of the constituent parts.

It is apparent, then, that the Constitution of a federation is likely to contain more elaborate and more complicated provisions in relation to the exercise of legislative power, and possibly also in relation to the exercise of executive and judicial power, than is the Constitution of a unitary state. But even here experience shows that it is possible to make this division of powers well and it is possible to make it badly. Indeed it is interesting to notice how often it is done badly and how hard it is to do it well. Consider first what looks like an elementary point. When a federal Constitution is being drawn up, is it best to set down a list of the matters over which the legislature of the whole country is to have exclusive authority, and leave the unenumerated remainder to the legislatures of the parts? Or is it better to enumerate the exclusive powers of the legislatures of the parts and leave the rest to the legislature of the whole? Or should there be two lists—one containing the exclusive powers of the whole and the other the exclusive powers of the parts? But this does not exhaust all the possibilities. May there not be some subjects upon which it is thought desirable that both legislatures should be entitled to make laws, though it would be understood that, if there was a conflict, the laws of one—normally the laws of the central legislature—should prevail? This idea of a concurrent jurisdiction occurs in most federal Constitutions and adds a possible third list to the other two.

If you look at the Constitution of India, 1950, which sets up a quasi-federal Constitution for India, you will find that the subjects over which the legislatures are to have authority are divided into three lists. There is a Union legislative list over which the legislature of the whole country has exclusive authority; there is a state legislative list over which the state legislatures have exclusive authority; and there is a concurrent legislative list over which both sets of legislatures have authority, with the proviso that state laws must, in general, give way to the laws of the central legislature on concurrent subjects if there is a conflict between them. In drafting the division of powers in this way, it is interesting to notice that the Indian framers of the Constitution of 1950 were following in the steps of the British draftsmen who drew up the Government of India Act, 1935, and who had provided there similarly three legislative lists. Indeed they had gone still further and had subdivided the concurrent list into two.

The Constitution of Canada also contains three lists, though it is true that the concurrent list is small—it contains only the two subjects of immigration and agriculture. The remaining two lists, however, illustrate very well the complications that must ensue when more than one list is adopted. It was apparently the intention of the framers of the Canadian Constitution that certain topics should be confided to the exclusive jurisdiction of the legislatures of the Provinces, and that the rest—with the exception of the small concurrent field already mentioned—should become the exclusive sphere of the Parliament of Canada. Accordingly, in section 92 of the Constitution, we find a list of subjects upon which, in each Province, the legislature may exclusively make laws. It would seem, surely, that the simplest thing to do then would be to say that the Parliament of Canada should have exclusive authority over all subjects not confided, by section 92, to the exclusive authority of the legislatures of the Provinces. The framers of the Constitution did in fact say this, but they were not content to stop at this. They went on to say, in words that have become famous as an example of unconscious irony, that 'for greater certainty' the powers of the Parliament of Canada extended to a list of subjects which they proceeded to enumerate.

But it may be asked what is the objection to having more than one list of subjects in a Constitution? The objection is that, from experience, it is certain that disputes will arise about whether a particular matter falls under the headings of one list or of the other, for words are wide and ambiguous, and it would be remarkable if, in drawing up two or three lists, there was not some possibility of overlapping between them. Canada has provided many examples of this, but it will be enough to quote the classic example. One topic which, in the Constitution, is handed over to the exclusive legislative authority of a Province is 'property and civil rights in the province'. At the same time the Parliament of Canada is given exclusive legislative authority over 'the regulation of trade and commerce' and 'banking, incorporation of banks and the issue of paper money'. Surely legislation on these topics is likely, in many cases, to affect 'property and civil rights in a province'? There has been a long series of disputes before the Canadian Courts upon the interpretation of this phrase and upon other apparent conflicts between the two lists in the Canadian Constitution. It is, indeed, difficult enough to interpret one list of subjects consistently. When a second or even a third is added the task of the Courts becomes most complicated and confused. It would seem, therefore, that a good rule in drawing up a Constitution for a federal state is to be content with but one list of subjects.

Whether this one list should contain the subjects upon which the central legislature should make laws, leaving the residue to the constituent units, or vice versa, is not easy to decide. It can be argued that it is better to specify the subjects within the authority of the units and leave the rest to the centre, because it is impossible to foresee what important subjects may arise in the future which the central legislature should control. A good example in this connexion is the development of aviation or of atomic energy. When the Constitutions of the United States, Switzerland, and Australia were drawn up the powers of the central legislature were specified and residual powers were left with the units, and, as at this time the developments of aviation and atomic energy were unknown, they find no explicit place in the list of central powers. In practice the position is not as bad as it sounds. Under the defence power and under power to regulate inter-state commerce and the like, the central legislatures have a good deal of power over these matters, but in Australia, for example, these powers are not complete and attempts have been made—unsuccessfully so far—to amend the Constitution to grant further powers over aviation to the parliament of the Commonwealth.

On the other hand, whatever may be the advantages of leaving future developments to be regulated by the central legislature, it proves in experience to be a fact that states or communities which are contemplating federal union prefer to set down explicitly and with limitations the matters which they are handing over to the central government. They are afraid of delivering a blank cheque. In some cases no federation at all could be formed unless the residual power was left with the federating units. Sometimes, too, no federation can be formed unless a concurrent list of subjects is adopted in addition to an exclusive list, and there may be occasions when three or more lists are required to satisfy the aspirations and scruples of those concerned. The Constitution maker has to weigh up the disadvantages of having a union on these complicated and inevitably troublesome terms and the disadvantages of having no union at all.

It may have been inferred from what has been said so far about the difficulties inherent in drafting a federal or quasi-federal Constitution that those who have to frame a Constitution for a unitary state may be assumed invariably to have a simple task. That is not correct. All that has been maintained is that in the framing of a federal Constitution difficult problems are bound to arise about what should or should not go into the Constitution because of the division of powers, and that these particular difficulties do not occur in the framing of a Constitution for a unitary state. But the framers of unitary Constitutions encounter troubles also—troubles which, it may be mentioned, sometimes confront the framers of federal Constitutions as well and add to their existing inevitable difficulties. The fact is that even when people agree that they want unitary government, they often believe that some restrictions should be placed upon the powers of that government. This attitude to government shows itself in the insertion into Constitutions of certain declarations of rights or liberties of the subject which it is intended that the government should enforce or at any rate not invade.

These declarations of rights provide a great problem for the maker of a Constitution. If they are not inserted, some influential body of opinion may be alienated and the Constitution may fail to be accepted. But if they are to be inserted it is extremely difficult to define the nature and extent of these rights in such a way that something significant and realistic is achieved. If a government is to be effective, few rights of its citizens can be stated in absolute form. If a Constitution declares that it guarantees to citizens, say freedom of speech, freedom of the press, freedom of assembly, freedom of street processions and demonstrations, and inviolability of the person and of the home, surely it guarantees licence. There must, it would seem, be some restrictions on these rights. Most Constitutions which contain declarations of rights do recognize that some qualifications must be attached to their exercise.

Among the few Constitutions which guarantee practically un-qualified rights to their citizens is that of the Soviet Union. In Article 125 of the Soviet Constitution of 1936 we read these words:

In accordance with the interests of the working people, and in order to strengthen the socialist system, the citizens of the U.S.S.R. are guaranteed by law:

(*a*) Freedom of speech;
(*b*) Freedom of the press;
(*c*) Freedom of assembly and meeting;
(*d*) Freedom of street processions and demonstrations.

These rights of citizens are ensured by placing at the disposal of the working people and their organizations printing shops, supplies of paper, public buildings, the streets, means of communication, and other material requisites for the exercise of these rights.

In Article 128 we read that 'the inviolability of the homes of citizens and secrecy of correspondence are protected by law'. But even in the Soviet Constitution some rights are subject to qualification. Article 127 guarantees to citizens 'inviolability of the person', but evidently the possibility of arrest is envisaged, for it adds: 'No one may be subject to arrest except by an order of the court or with the sanction of a state attorney.'

The Constitution of the Federal Peoples Republic of Jugoslavia (1946), which has many family resemblances to the Soviet Con-stitution, also includes an unqualified guarantee (in Article 27) of freedom of the press, of speech, of association, of assembly, and of public meeting. But in other respects it is less generous in bestowing freedom upon the citizens. It envisages the possibility of arrest, according to the law, as the Soviet Constitution does, but it falls short of the Soviet Constitution in its guarantees of inviolability of the home and secrecy of correspondence. Articles 29 and 30 explain that the production of a legal search warrant will authorize entering another person's premises, and that in cases of criminal inquiry, mobilization, or war, the privacy of means of communication will not be absolute.

No realistic attempt to define the rights of the citizen, indeed, can fail to include qualifications. Yet when we see the result it is difficult to resist asking the question: What of substance is left after the qualifications have been given full effect? The Constitution of Ireland provides an interesting example of this position. It contains a series of articles—numbers 40–44—enunciating fundamental rights. Consider this statement first: 'No citizen shall be deprived of his personal liberty save in accordance with law.' A little later there follows: 'The dwelling of every citizen is inviolable and shall not be forcibly entered save in accordance with law.' What does this guarantee amount to? The answer must be: 'It all depends on the law.' If wide discretionary powers of arrest and forcible entry are given by the law to the forces of the state, then the right of the citizen will be severely restricted.

The experience of Ireland in the years immediately following the adoption of the Constitution in 1937 illustrates the dilemma very well. In 1940 the Irish parliament passed the Offences Against the State (Amendment) Act, section 4 of which ran as follows: 'Whenever a Minister of State is of opinion that any particular person is engaged in activities which, in his opinion, are prejudicial to the preservation of public peace and order, or to the security of the State, such Minister may by warrant under his hand and sealed with his official seal, order the arrest and detention of such person. . . .' The Supreme Court of Ireland was asked to decide whether or not this and certain other provisions of this Act were valid, in that they appeared to conflict with the guarantee of certain rights contained in the Constitution. It decided that the Act was valid. It directed its attention particularly to the declaration in the Constitution (Article 40 (3)) that the State guarantees by its laws to respect, and, as far as practicable, by its laws to defend and vindicate the personal rights of the citizen, and to protect from unjust attack and, in case of injustice done, to vindicate, the life, person, good name, and property rights of every citizen. The Supreme Court declared that the Act was not repugnant to this clause. 'The duty', it said, 'of determining the extent to which the rights of any particular citizen, or class of citizens, can properly be harmonized with the rights of the citizens as a whole seems to us to be a matter which is peculiarly within the province of the Oireachtas [Legislature], and any attempt by this Court to control the Oireachtas in the exercise of this function, would, in our opinion, be a usurpation of its authority.' It went on to discuss the phrase 'in accordance with the law'. It said: 'The phrase "in accordance with the law" is used in several Articles of the Constitution, and we are of opinion that it means in accordance with the law as it exists at the time when the particular Article is invoked and sought to be applied. . . . A person in custody is detained in accordance with law if he is detained in accordance with the provisions of a statute duly passed by the Oireachtas; subject always to the qualification that such provisions are not repugnant to the Constitution or to any provision thereof.' (In re *Offences Against the State (Amendment) Bill, 1940* [1940] I.R. 470 at pp. 481-2.)

The declaration of rights in this form is commonly found in Constitutions. Thus Article 7 of the Belgian Constitution guarantees individual liberty, but it goes on to say that no one may be arrested except upon a warrant, unless taken in the act of committing an offence. A similar provision is found in the Constitutions of Holland (Art. 164), Norway (Art. 99), Sweden (Art. 16), and Denmark (Art. 78). The Danish Constitution makes precise stipulations about the right of an arrested person to be brought before a judge within twenty-four hours, and to have the lawfulness of his arrest determined. These countries have a reputation for good government; they exhibit few traces of the arbitrary exercise of power. It may be asserted that these and similar declarations in their Constitutions of rights which may not be restricted except in accordance with the law, are in practice effective, because the law confers no arbitrary powers upon the executive. The law in Soviet Russia or in Jugoslavia is not so restrictive of the powers of the executive.

It is fair to emphasize the object which those who insert a declaration of rights in these terms have in view. They hope by asserting that rights may not be restricted, save in accordance with the law, that the exercise of arbitrary power may be abolished or greatly reduced in the state. They hope that in consequence nobody may be arrested by the mere unauthorized action of another. Lawful authority must be invoked for any violation of rights. They would probably argue that any wide grant by the legislature of uncontrolled powers of arrest, detention, or suppression to the executive is not government according to law in fact, though it may be so in form. Law, they would say, means regulation according to principles and rules; it does not mean the mere passing of enabling acts which permit the executive to do as it pleases.

Yet when all is said and done, this phrase 'save in accordance with the law' can be an empty promise. It appears to reach its most absurd form in a passage in the declaration of rights found in the Preamble to the Constitution of the Fourth French Republic, where it is written: 'The right to strike may be exercised within the framework of the laws that govern it.' It must be emphasized strongly that the extent to which rights can be guaranteed and preserved under this formula will depend in the last resort upon the restraint of the legislature.

Attempts are made in most Constitutions, however, to face the difficulties involved in inserting a declaration of rights and not to dodge them always by the employment of some such phrase as 'save in accordance with the law'. Here the Irish and the Indian Constitutions provide some examples which illustrate how hard it is to do the thing satisfactorily. We may take our examples from the Irish Constitution. In Article 40 (6) of the Constitution it is declared that the State guarantees liberty for the exercise of the 'right of the citizens to express freely their convictions and opinions', 'the right of the citizens to assemble peaceably and without arms', and 'the right of the citizens to form associations and unions'. But the framers of the Constitution felt obliged to qualify the whole guarantee of liberty by the phrase 'subject to public order and morality'. The right to express opinion freely is made subject to the proviso that 'the State shall endeavour to ensure that organs of public opinion, such as the radio, the press, the cinema, while preserving their rightful liberty of expression, including criticism of Government policy, shall not be used to undermine public order or morality or the authority of the State', and it is declared that the publication or utterance of blasphemous, seditious, or indecent matter is an offence which shall be punishable in accordance with law. The declaration of the right to assemble peaceably is followed by a proviso that meetings calculated to cause a breach of the peace or to be a danger or a nuisance may be controlled or prevented; meetings held in the vicinity of either House of the legislature may similarly be controlled or prevented. The right of association is similarly declared to be subject to regulation and control by law in the public interest. Similar guarantees of rights with similar restrictions are found in Articles 19 to 22 of the Indian Constitution. Most people would agree that these restrictions upon the rights concerned are not unreasonable. They are part of the law in many countries in the British Commonwealth, though these countries seldom include declarations of rights in their Constitutions. Does the qualified enactment of these rights in the Irish or Indian Constitutions accomplish anything?

A classic example of giving a right with one hand and taking it back with the other may be found in Article 43 of the Irish Constitution, which deals with the right of private property. The Article begins with these encouraging words: 'The State acknowledges that man, in virtue of his rational being, has the natural right, antecedent to positive law, to the private ownership of external goods.' It continues with a clause calculated to lift up the heart of the most old-fashioned capitalist: 'The State accordingly guarantees to pass no law attempting to abolish the right of private ownership or the general right to transfer, bequeath and inherit property.' But the next two sentences are likely to disappoint: 'The State recognizes, however, that the exercise of the rights mentioned in the foregoing provisions of this Article ought, in civil society, to be regulated by the principles of social justice. The State, accordingly, may as occasion requires, delimit by law the exercise of the said rights with a view to reconciling their exercise with the exigencies of the common good.' The Constitution of Jugoslavia goes hardly further than this when, in Article 18, having asserted that private property and private initiative in economy are guaranteed, it goes on to declare that 'private property may be limited or expropriated, if the common interest requires it, but only in accordance with the law'. Few expectations are aroused and few disappointed in the formula adopted by Article 10 of the Soviet Constitution of 1936: 'The right of personal property of citizens in their income from work and in their savings, in their dwelling house and tools, in household articles and utensils, and in articles for personal use and comfort, as well as the right of inheritance of personal property of citizens, is protected by law.'

If rights are defined and guaranteed in these vague and contradictory terms—and it is almost impossible to define them otherwise—how difficult it is to enforce the observance of these provisions. How can the extent of a right declared in such terms be determined? The problem is of little importance in countries where declarations of rights are regarded as no more than rhetoric or subterfuge, but when an honest attempt is made in practice in a country to give effect to rights guaranteed in the Constitution, difficulties arise. In some cases it is open to the citizen to challenge in a court of law an act of the executive or of the legislature on the ground that it infringes rights guaranteed to him by the Constitution. But when the words of the Constitution are so vague and qualified, and when also they are charged with emotional or political content, the task imposed upon the judges comes near to being one which the judiciary cannot discharge without involving itself in current controversy.

Here the experience of the United States provides some revealing examples. The first ten amendments of the American Constitution, which were adopted *en bloc* in 1791, are usually called 'the Bill of rights' and they, along with other provisions of the Constitution itself and other amendments, assert and undertake to protect certain rights of the citizen, particularly against the government. The interpretation of these provisions, in a number of disputed cases, has been the duty of the Supreme Court of the United States, and it has been obliged to give a precise meaning to such phrases as 'the free exercise of religion', 'freedom of speech or of the press', and, most difficult of all perhaps, the provision that no person shall be 'deprived of life, liberty, or property, without due process of law; nor shall private property be taken for public use, without just compensation'.

These are vague terms. 'Liberty' means different things to different people and to the same people at different times. In 1940 the Supreme Court of the United States was asked to decide on the validity of a regulation of a school board in the State of Pennsylvania which required children attending the State schools to participate in a ceremony of saluting the American flag. (*Minersville School District*

v. *Gobitis* 310 U.S. 586.) Some children of parents who belonged to the sect known as 'Jehovah's Witnesses' had refused to salute the American flag on the ground that to do so was in conflict with their religious beliefs. The Supreme Court was asked to declare that the regulation was invalid because it attempted to prohibit the free exercise of religion. The Court decided, with only one dissentient, that the regulation was valid. The argument of the majority was that the regulation, in requiring a ceremony of respect for the flag, was attempting, however unwisely, to strengthen the foundations of American society, and thus, so far from infringing liberty, was supporting the basis upon which it existed. The Court refused to substitute its own judgement of what was desirable in a matter of this kind for the judgement of the legislature. The dissenting judge Mr Justice (later Chief Justice) Stone declared that the regulation was so clear a violation of liberty, both of speech and religion as guaranteed by this Constitution, that the Court was entitled to declare it invalid. In 1942, however, in the course of deciding a case, also brought by the Jehovah's Witnesses, concerning the validity of a requirement in the ordinances of certain American cities that sellers of various articles including books should be licensed, three of the judges of the Supreme Court, Justices Black, Douglas, and Murphy, said that they had come to the conclusion that their view in the earlier case involving the saluting of the flag was wrong. (*Jones* v. *Opelika* 316 U.S. 584 at pp. 623–4.) A year later, the decision in the case of 1940 was overruled, though by a majority. (*West Virginia Board of Education* v. *Barnette* 319 U.S. 624.) It may be mentioned that two new judges sat on the Court in 1943, as compared with the Court of 1940, and that Mr. Justice Stone was now Chief Justice. No one need be surprised that judges find it difficult to agree or to be consistent or certain in their interpretation of words of this kind.

'Liberty' in the economic sphere may legitimately be used in different senses. One man may say that economic liberty means that a man may sell his labour for what he can get for it and work for as long as he can; another will say that, in the world as it is, many men will be unable to sell their labour at all unless some restrictions are placed upon maximum hours of labour and minimum rates of wages. The first view we associate with *laissez-faire*, the second with the age of collectivism. The Supreme Court of the United States has not been unaffected by the changes in opinion in that country during the first half of the twentieth century. In 1905 (in the case of *Lochner* v. *New York* 198 U.S. 45) the Court declared that a statute of New York State which had fixed a maximum of sixty hours per week and ten hours per day for bakers was invalid, on the ground that it violated the liberty of the citizen to work as long as he liked. The right to sell or purchase labour, the Court said, was part of the liberty which the Constitution guaranteed. But it is interesting to notice that this view prevailed by a majority of five to four—the Court was far from unanimous. In 1908, however, the Court unanimously sustained an act of the State of Oregon fixing a maximum of ten hours a day for women workers in certain employments (*Muller* v. *Oregon* 208 U.S. 412), and in 1917, by a majority of five to three, it sustained an act of the same state extending the maximum of ten hours to men (*Bunting* v. *Oregon* 243 U.S. 426).

Many cases of this kind can be discovered in the history of the Supreme Court of the United States, and something more will be said of the problems facing judges in their task of interpreting a Constitution in Chapter 7. What deserves emphasis at this stage is that the introduction of declarations of rights into a Constitution in vague terms, and with considerable room for legitimate difference of opinion, places a difficult responsibility upon judges. If Courts attempt to evade the task of interpreting these phrases and insist more and more that it is for the legislature to decide what constitutes 'liberty' or 'just compensation' or 'free speech' or 'the safety of the state' or 'public welfare'—and there is a strong tendency for Courts to take this line as the judgement of the Supreme Court of the United States in the case of 1940 illustrates—then it may well be asked what sanction lies behind these declarations of rights. Do we not come back again to reliance upon the self-restraint of the legislature or the controlling power of public opinion? One lesson at least seems clear. If there must be such declarations, let the language be clear and precise.

An appreciation of the difficulties which arise if Courts are asked to enforce or apply declarations of rights in a Constitution has led sometimes to a decision by the framers of a Constitution that the declaration of some rights at any rate shall not be regarded as a collection of rules of law in the sense that Courts are to be asked to recognize and apply them, but rather as a statement of desirable objectives. This plan was adopted in the Irish Constitution and followed by the framers of the Indian Constitution. Thus in the Irish Constitution there is an Article—No. 45—headed 'Directive Principles of Social Policy', and it is expressly stated at the beginning of this Article that the principles set forth in it are intended for the general guidance of the Legislature. 'The application of those principles in the making of laws shall be the care of the Legislature (Oireachtas) exclusively, and shall not be cognizable by any Court under any of the provisions of this Constitution.' Similar provisions are found in Part IV of the Indian Constitution under the heading 'Directive Principles of State Policy'. This means that if any citizen believes that a law passed by the legislature or the failure of the legislature to pass a law conflicts with one of these directive principles, he may not seek in a Court to get that law declared invalid or to get a writ directed to the legislature to require them to pass a law. When one peruses the terms of these Articles one cannot deny that it would be foolish to allow Courts to concern themselves with these matters. What is difficult to understand, however, is why, if these provisions are removed from the cognizance of the Courts, others equally vague are apparently within the ambit of the Courts.

It may be doubted whether there is any gain, on balance, from introducing these paragraphs of generalities into a Constitution anywhere at all, if it is intended that the Constitution should command the respect as well as the affection of the people. If the Constitution is to be taken seriously, the interpretation and fulfilment of these general objects of policy will raise great difficulties for Courts and for legislatures, and these difficulties will bring the Constitution, the Courts, and the legislatures into conflict and disrepute. If these declarations are, however, to be neglected, if they are to be treated as 'words', they will bring discredit upon the Constitution also.

This is not to say that there is no place whatever for a guarantee of certain rights in a Constitution. The experience of the United States in this matter is instructive. Although the American Constitution enunciated certain limitations upon government in terms which were vague, it has also set an example by declaring certain rights in careful and precise language. Amendment XV reads: 'The right of citizens of the United States to vote shall not be denied or abridged by the United States or by any State on account of race, colour, or previous condition of servitude.'

Nothing could be clearer than this language. Yet the history of the United States from 1870, when Amendment XV came into effect, until this day, illustrates how difficult it is to ensure that rights, even when declared in language so clear and unambiguous as this, can be effectively exercised in a community which is apathetic or hostile to them. It is well known that the right of the negro to vote in certain of the Southern States in the American Union is, in practice, seldom exercised. When attempts are made to restrict its exercise by law it has been possible to test the validity of such laws in the Supreme Court of the United States, and many State laws have been declared invalid by this process. In the last analysis, however, the exercise of these rights depends upon the willingness of a community to tolerate or protect them, and this willingness is absent in many Southern States.

The United States illustrates very well the dilemma in which Constitution makers are placed when they consider this question of a declaration of rights. If they are framing a Constitution for people who are likely to respect rights, then a hard and fast declaration of rights in a Constitution is hardly necessary—their recognition in the ordinary law would be more flexible and just as effective. If on the other hand they are framing a Constitution for people who are not likely to respect rights, will the enunciation of certain rights in the Constitution go far towards ensuring their effective exercise? Would it not be better to proceed slowly by the process of ordinary law and by persuasion?

The experience of the United States shows that no certain answer can be given to this question. Historians would differ, but it can be asserted with some justification that the declaration of rights in Amendment XV, for example, has done something, if only something negative, to protect the negro's status. It has permitted appeals to the Supreme Court to invalidate State legislation; it has also empowered Congress to legislate in order to enforce these rights in the States. It is admitted that action by the Supreme Court or by Congress or by the executive can go a short way only; the final guarantee of the exercise of the right of the negro to vote in the

Southern States rests on the formation of a favourable public opinion in those States. Yet it could not be asserted that the declaration in the Constitution was worthless. At the same time, to the extent to which the guarantees of the Constitution are plainly known to be ineffective or inoperative, to that extent its strength and sanctity are impaired.

If these things can happen in a country like the United States where respect for the Constitution and for the Supreme Court is strong; where the words of the Constitution, vague as they are at times, are interpreted not by the executive but by the Court; and where public opinion is articulate and organized; how much more likely is it that declarations of rights may prove to be in practice little more than words in communities where the executive is held in greater awe than the Constitution, where people are not free to organize themselves or where they lack knowledge and capacity to form a public opinion.

The ideal Constitution, then, would contain few or no declarations of rights, though the ideal system of law would define and guarantee many rights. Rights cannot be declared in a Constitution except in absolute and unqualified terms, unless indeed they are so qualified as to be meaningless—and we have seen many examples of this. It is in the ordinary law itself that the careful definition of rights can be best undertaken, with the added guarantee that the law, since it has been passed by a legislature, may in most cases be in line with dominant public opinion.

To confine a Constitution to the bare statement of the rules which establish the principal political institutions of the State may seem unduly austere. Let it be said at once that a preamble to a Constitution, which is not itself part of the Constitution and therefore not part of the law, is not only permissible but even desirable. In this respect the framers of the American Constitution set an admirable example when, in 1787, they prefaced their document with this one compact and eloquent sentence: 'We, the people of the United States, in order to form a more perfect Union, establish justice, insure domestic tranquillity, provide for the common defence, promote the general welfare, and secure the blessings of liberty to ourselves and our posterity, do ordain and establish this Constitution for the United States of America.' The framers of the Constitution of the Fifth French Republic dealt with the problem of a declaration of rights—an historic and traditional part of French Constitution making—by placing it in the preamble to the Constitution and contenting themselves with proclaiming 'their attachment to the Rights of Man and the principles of National Sovereignty'.

Most Constitutions have some preamble. Those manufactured by the British parliament for the overseas countries of the Commonwealth are usually strictly factual, narrating the steps by which the act has come to be passed. Other countries permit themselves more emotion and eloquence. Most ascribe sovereignty to the people. Ireland invokes the name of 'the Most Holy Trinity from Whom is all authority and to Whom, as our final end, all actions both of men and States must be referred'; Switzerland begins with the words *Au Nom de Dieu Tout-Puissant*. The Soviet Constitution dispenses with a preamble.

But while a preamble is right and proper, it is worth remarking that a Constitution is, first of all, a legal document. It is intended to state supreme rules of law. It should confine itself, therefore, as completely as possible to stating rules of law, not opinions, aspirations, directives, and policies. Moreover, if it is to state rules of law and if, in particular, those rules are to constitute supreme law, binding the legislature equally with the executive and judiciary—and this is the avowed intention of most Constitutions, as we have seen—then these rules should be few, they should be general, and they should be fundamental. They should relate to subjects which it is fitting and proper to attempt to describe and regulate in terms of a rule of law. Finally, the language employed, though inevitably general and wide in some matters, should at the same time avoid so far as possible the ambiguous, the emotional, and the tendentious.

If it is desired that a Constitution should evoke not only the respect due to law but also the added reverence due to a supreme law, then surely it is wise to exclude from its confines, as completely as possible, anything that is not intended to be regarded as a rule of law. This, at any rate, is the way in which a Constitution is viewed by those brought up and trained in what may be called the English view of constitutional law. But not all writers on Constitutions would accept this view. For many people a Constitution is something more than a selection of supreme legal rules. It is often, and sometimes first, a political manifesto or creed or testament. As such, it can be argued, it evokes the respect and affection and, indeed, obedience of the people in a way which no exclusively legal document can hope to do. It is interesting, therefore, to turn now to consider just what authority a Constitution can claim.

4

What Authority a Constitution can Claim

IN THE COURSE OF the acute controversy which raged in the years before the outbreak of the American Civil War, William Henry Seward, a leading opponent of slavery, declared in the Senate of the United States: 'There is a higher law than the Constitution.' The phrase, torn from its context, was seized upon by both the opponents and the defenders of slavery. Its implication for them was that even if the Constitution recognized and protected slavery, its provisions need not be regarded as binding by those who were opposed to slavery. It was an implication which undermined both the legal and the moral authority of the Constitution. Seward was opening up the whole question, a fundamental question, of what authority a Constitution can claim. It is a legal question and a moral question. It will be best to start with some discussion of the legal question.

In what circumstances can a Constitution claim to have legal authority? By what criteria do those whose business it is to administer the law, and particularly those who administer law in the Courts, recognize that a certain document, described as a Constitution, is part of the law? The general answer to this question is that it must have been enacted or approved or promulgated by a body recognized as competent to make law. But can there be a body competent to make law before a Constitution is in being? Do not Constitutions themselves create law-making bodies? Clearly it becomes necessary to conceive of a body which can give force of law to a Constitution before the Constitution itself authorizes the setting up of law-making bodies. Who are these original, primeval law-givers? To this question different answers are given in different communities.

Let us begin with what appears a relatively simple case. Some of the Constitutions in the countries of the British Commonwealth owe their legal validity to the fact that they were enacted or promulgated either by the parliament of the United Kingdom at Westminster, or by the Queen in Council, or under the authority of one or other of these two bodies. It is recognized as a rule of law in most parts of the British Commonwealth that the parliament at Westminster and, in some cases, the Queen in Council have power to make laws extending to the overseas parts of the Commonwealth and possessing full force of law there. If we ask, then, by what criterion the Constitutions of Australia or Trinidad, of New Zealand or Malta, of Ceylon, of Canada, or of Jamaica are recognized to be law in those countries, the answer is that they were, from the legal point of view, made in Britain. Their legal authority comes from a law-giver which existed before they did and which is external to themselves. That is a lawyer's answer to the question: What legal authority can the Constitution of a British Dominion or of a colony claim? It can claim the authority, which lawyers regard as sufficient, of an act of parliament of the United Kingdom or of an Order in Council.

But not all countries in the British Commonwealth have been content to rely for the legal authority of their Constitution upon its carrying the imprint 'Made in England'. The Irish, when they came to draw up a Constitution for themselves in 1922, soon came into conflict with this doctrine. They elected a body in 1922 which drew up a Constitution for the Irish Free State. This assembly claimed that it drew its authority from God and the people of Ireland and it proceeded, as it said, 'in the exercise of undoubted right' to decree and enact that the Constitution which it had drawn up 'shall be the Constitution of the Irish Free State'. In the view of the members of this assembly the Constitution had force of law because they had enacted it, and their authority to enact it came from the people. On the British side this claim was not accepted. In the British view the body which drew up the Constitution had been elected under the authority of an act of parliament at Westminster— the Irish Free State Agreement Act, 1922—and it had no power to enact a Constitution. Once the Constitution had been prepared by the Irish assembly, it was necessary, if it was to have force of law in Ireland, for it to be approved and legalized by the parliament at Westminster. This was accordingly done by the Irish Free State Constitution Act, 1922, which in its preamble clearly indicated what it thought of the pretensions of the Irish body to enact a Constitution by referring to what that body had prepared as 'a measure', not 'an act', and explicitly describing the Irish assembly as 'constituted pursuant to the Irish Free State Agreement Act'. These two views of the source of authority for the Irish Constitution cannot be reconciled. Nor is it necessary for our purposes to discuss which has the greater merit in law. Their interest lies in the fact that the framers of the Constitution of the Irish Free State attempted to introduce into the constitutional law of the Commonwealth a law-giver which was—and is—unknown to British law, namely the people.

In 1937 the Irish drew up a new Constitution and on this occasion their position was less ambiguous. The draft Constitution was approved by their parliament but not enacted, so that it was impossible to assert that it received force of law from a parliament which in its turn originally received authority from the parliament at Westminster. Instead, after approval by the Irish parliament, it was submitted to the people, and upon receiving their approval by a majority, had force of law in Eire. And it boldly declares at the outset: 'We, the people of Eire, . . . do hereby adopt, enact, and give to ourselves this Constitution.'

Eire left the British Commonwealth in 1949, but the Constitution of India of 1950 makes the same claim that its authority is derived from the people. It, too, begins with the words: 'We, the people of India, . . . in our Constituent Assembly this twenty-sixth day of November, 1949, do hereby adopt, enact and give to ourselves this Constitution.' 'We, the people.' The phrase takes us back to the first of the modern Constitutions and the oldest Constitution still in operation. It was with this phrase that the Americans opened their fine preamble to their Constitution: 'We the people of the United States . . . do ordain and establish this Constitution for the United States.'

Most modern Constitutions have followed the American model and the legal and political theory that lies behind it. The people, or a constituent assembly acting on their behalf, has authority to enact a Constitution. This statement is regarded as no mere flourish. It is accepted as law. The Courts of the Irish Free State spoke of the Constitution of 1922 as having been enacted by the people, and the Courts of Eire speak in the same way of the Constitution of 1937. The Supreme Court of the United States regards the people as having given force of law to the Constitution. In an early case, *McCulloch* v. *Maryland* in 1819 (4 Wheaton 316), Chief Justice Marshall said: 'The government proceeds directly from the people; is "ordained and established" in the name of the people; ... In form and in substance it emanates from them. Its powers are granted by them, and are to be exercised directly on them, and for their benefit. ... It is the government of all; its powers are delegated by all; it represents all, and acts for all.'

A high point in the history of the people as the law-giver came after the First World War when new Constitutions were adopted upon the defeat of the German, Russian, and Austro-Hungarian Empires. Each new Constitution declared that it received force of law from the people. The Weimar Constitution began: 'The German people, ... has given itself this Constitution.' The same sort of phrase occurs in the other Constitutions. 'We, the Czechoslovak nation, ... have adopted the following Constitution for the Czecho-slovak Republic.' 'The Estonian people . . . has drawn up and accepted through the Constituent Assembly the Constitution as follows.' 'We, the Polish nation, . . . do enact and establish in the Legislative Sjem of the Republic of Poland this constitutional law.' After the Second World War there was not the same emphasis upon the power of the people to enact a Constitution. In the Constitution of the Fourth French Republic the sovereignty of the people is declared, but it is exercised through the institutions which the Constitution establishes, and the people's part in bringing the Con-stitution into force is described by the sentence 'The French people has approved'. The Constitution of Jugoslavia of 1946 is enacted by the Constituent Assembly. In the Constitution of the West German Federal Republic, however, it is declared that 'the German people has, by virtue of its constituent power, enacted this basic law of the Federal Republic of Germany'.

What seems to emerge from an examination of Constitutions is that, from the strictly legal point of view, they have legal authority because they have been enacted by a body recognized as competent to give them force of law. This body is either some external legislative body like the parliament of the United Kingdom or it is the people of the territory or it is a constituent assembly chosen in some way, often by the people, and recognized to have authority to establish a Constitution.

Before we examine the significance of these explanations, it is perhaps better to take our inquiries a little further. Most Constitutions claim to possess the authority not of law only but of supreme law. How is this claim justified? By what argument can it be said that the law in a Constitution is superior to the law enacted by legislative authorities established in a country by the Constitution? And, let it be stressed, it is only as a matter of law that we are asking this question at this stage.

There are two main types of answer to this question. The first may be described as an answer based upon the logic of the situation. It asserts that from the very nature of a Constitution it must follow that it has superiority over the institutions which it creates. That is the whole idea of a Constitution. It is not just an ordinary law. It is often prior in time to the legislature, but even if it is not, it is logically prior. Its function is to regulate institutions, to govern a government. It cannot be construed in the same way and upon the same principles as a law to regulate the licensing of dogs.

Once again some words used by Chief Justice Marshall, this time in the case of *Marbury* v. *Madison* in 1803 (1 Cranch 137), express this argument as cogently as possible. He said:

Certainly all those who have framed written constitutions contemplate them as forming the fundamental and paramount law of the nation, and, consequently, the theory of every such government must be, that an act of the legislature, repugnant to the constitution, is void.

To what purpose are powers limited, and to what purpose is that limitation committed to writing, if these limits may, at any time, be passed by those intended to be restrained? The distinction between a government with limited and unlimited powers is abolished, if those limits do not confine the persons upon whom they are imposed, and if acts prohibited and acts allowed are of equal obligation. It is a proposition too plain to be contested, that the Constitution controls any legislative act repugnant to it; or, that the legislature may alter the Constitution by an ordinary act. Between these alternatives there is no middle ground. The Constitution is either a superior, paramount law, unchangeable by ordinary means, or it is on a level with ordinary legislative acts, and, like other acts, is alterable when the legislature shall please to alter it. If the former part of the alternative be true, then a legislative act contrary to the Constitution is not law; if the latter part be true, then written Constitutions are absurd attempts, on the part of the people, to limit a power in its own nature illimitable.

On this argument, if a Constitution claims, by its terms, to limit the powers of the institutions it creates, including the legislature, its provisions must surely be regarded as of superior force to any rules or actions issuing from those institutions. To think otherwise reduces a Constitution and the business of Constitution-making to nonsense.

Another line of argument by which the supremacy in law of a Constitution is demonstrated is that the Constitution is the product of a body which has power to make supreme law. Here there re-appear once more the three principal bodies which we encountered earlier—the external, supreme legislature, like the British parliament, or the people, or a constituent assembly.

So far as most of the Constitutions within the British Commonwealth are concerned they have the force of superior law and they obtain that force from the fact that they were enacted by the British parliament or by the Queen in Council. For such enactment not only gives force of law to a Constitution, but also such force that the law of the Constitution is of higher status than law made by any local legislature. If we ask, therefore, why the Constitution of the Commonwealth of Australia is supreme over the parliament of the Commonwealth and indeed limits both the government of the Commonwealth and the governments of the States, the answer is that it is supreme because it is an act of the parliament of the United Kingdom. That is the rule that is accepted by the Courts in Australia.

Until 1931 it was the accepted rule of interpretation throughout the British Empire that the parliament of the United Kingdom could make laws extending to the overseas Dominions and Colonies if it thought fit, and that if it did so, these laws were of supreme force in those territories. With the gradual development of equal status between the United Kingdom and the Dominions, however, it was thought that something should be done to reconcile this legal supremacy of the parliament in Britain with the desire of the Dominions to be self-governing in law as well as in fact. As part of the measures necessary to achieve this end there was passed in 1931 the Statute of Westminster, the effect of which was to record an understanding that the parliament of the United Kingdom would not make laws extending to a Dominion except at the request and with the consent of that Dominion, and, what was more, that any act of the parliament of the United Kingdom which did extend to a Dominion should be capable of amendment by the parliament of the Dominion. This meant that henceforth laws made at Westminster for the Dominions would be placed on an equal footing with laws made by the legislatures in the Dominions themselves. The old quality of supremacy or superiority would be circumvented.

If this principle had been applied to the Dominions without qualification it was feared that a startling result would have followed. The Constitutions of the Dominions, all of them acts of the British parliament, would have been placed on an equal footing with laws made by the Dominion parliaments. They would have been capable of alteration by the ordinary legislative process. They would cease to be supreme, in so far as their supremacy had been based upon a peculiar quality attaching to legislation of the United Kingdom parliament which the Statute of Westminster had now made it possible to overcome. This result did not alarm all the Dominions. The Union of South Africa in particular was quite prepared to accept a situation in which its Constitution lost any superior force which it had obtained from its status of being in origin an act of the parliament of the United Kingdom. But New Zealand, Canada, and Australia were anxious to make no change. In the case of New Zealand there was a conservative desire to leave things as they were and it was not until 1947 that the Constitution of New Zealand lost its supreme quality and became capable of alteration by the ordinary process of legislation in the New Zealand parliament. Canada and Australia were in a different position from New Zealand. For one thing they possessed federal Constitutions whereas New Zealand's Constitution was unitary. It was essential for them, therefore, to maintain the supremacy of their Constitutions. In order to keep their Constitutions supreme they decided that the terms of the Statute of

Westminster should not extend to them so far as the amendment of the Constitutions was concerned. In the outcome, therefore, the Statute of Westminster has been applied to the Dominions, but in the case of Canada and Australia a special exception was made in the Statute to exclude the Constitutions from its operation.

It has been thought proper to enter into a little detail upon this question because the experience of the Dominions as they have obtained self-government has brought to the fore the problem: How can a Constitution be endowed with supreme legal authority? Upon what can such a claim be based? Under the old order when the supremacy of legislation produced by the United Kingdom was un-questioned, no difficulty in law arose. But when self-government came to be achieved, obstacles arose. Did it not seem that, if a Dominion wished to have a supreme Constitution, it could do so only if it was content to allow its Constitution to carry upon it still the mark: 'Made in Britain'? And yet was that not rather a denial of complete self-government in the legal sense? In fact Canada and Australia have so far accepted this apparent contradiction. The supremacy of their Constitutions in law rests upon the fact that they were enacted by an external legislature whose enactments in Canada and Australia are of superior force to those made by any legislature in Canada or Australia.

It may be thought that the problem raised here is only of academic interest. In fact, however, it is a consideration which is of some weight in satisfying the nationalistic aspirations of members of the British Commonwealth. For some people it is not enough to be self-governing and independent in practice; they must be seen to be so in law also. In the case of South Africa the problem might have become difficult had they desired to maintain the supremacy of the Constitution. But what could be done if Canada or Australia wished, while retaining supreme Constitutions, to be rid of the marks of legal inferiority to the parliament of the United Kingdom? Two possibilities can be suggested. The first is that they might adopt the line of argument which we described at the outset—the logical argument, the argument of Chief Justice Marshall in *Marbury* v. *Madison*. Their Constitutions could be placed upon the same footing in law as any other law, but it would be accepted by the Courts that because the Constitutions established the institutions of government and imposed limitations upon them, therefore those limitations must be enforced. The Constitutions would be given a priority over other laws, a logical priority based upon their terms and upon the nature of a Constitution. This would be a reasonable line of interpretation and perhaps not entirely novel, for it would represent really an extension—though admittedly a large extension—of principles already applied in judicial interpretation. It would certainly involve no break in legal history.

The second possible course would involve a break, if not, in the legal sense, a revolution. They might decide to base the legal supremacy of the Constitution upon the will of the people or of a constituent assembly itself authorized by the people to draw up a Constitution. That, after all, is one of the arguments upon which the supremacy in law of the American Constitution is based. Not only can its supremacy be based upon the logical argument of Chief Justice Marshall in *Marbury* v. *Madison* but also it can be argued that the law which the people give is superior to the law which its agents, the government set up by the people's will, can enact. This position was well stated by Alexander Hamilton in *The Federalist* when he said: 'There is no position which depends on clearer principles than that every act of a delegated authority, contrary to the tenor of the commission under which it is exercised, is void. No legislative act, therefore, contrary to the Constitution can be valid. To deny this would be to affirm that the deputy is greater than his principal; that the servant is above his master, that the representatives of the people are superior to the people themselves; that men acting by virtue of powers may do not only what their powers do not authorize, but what they forbid.' And he concludes that 'the Constitution ought to be preferred to the Statute, the intention of the people to the intention of their agents'.

There is no doubt that the supremacy of the people as law-giver is recognized in the United States so far as the Constitution is concerned. It is accepted, indeed, in most countries. To introduce it into the law of the British Commonwealth, however, is an innovation. The people there, so far from being a supreme law-giver, is not, as was pointed out above, a law-giver at all. Yet already the innovation has been made. The supremacy of the Indian Constitution of 1950 and of the Irish Constitution of 1937 arises from the fact that it claims to be the work of the people. In the case of India the Constitution was not actually referred to the people for its approval, and it declares itself, therefore, in the preamble to be enacted by the people in their constituent assembly. But the Irish Constitution was in fact submitted in a referendum to the people and it came into force as a result of their approval.

Why should not other members of the Commonwealth follow this example? Although Eire has since left the Commonwealth, India's continuing membership of it, even as a republic, has been accepted and endorsed by the other members whose Constitutions obtain their legal validity and their supremacy, where it exists, from enactment not by the people but by the parliament of the United Kingdom. Evidently, as a matter of politics, it can be done and it may be done again. As a matter of law, however, it is clear that it involves a break with the past. That break is not so noticeable if a member of the Commonwealth becomes a republic because, when it does that, it ceases to be part of the Queen's dominions and therefore lies outside the jurisdiction of the parliament of the United Kingdom. But if, say, Canada wished to remain a kingdom and at the same time wished its Constitution to possess legal supremacy by virtue only of the will of the Canadian people, it would involve a break in legal continuity within what, in law, would still be one legal entity. From these discussions, however, it is clear that the law is made to fit the national aspirations of communities, and that if it should prove necessary within the British Commonwealth, radical changes in legal conceptions will be made, and the law forced into line with dominant desires.

It will be noticed that many of these legal conceptions seem to be legal fictions. 'The people' enact the Constitution of Eire, yet in fact it was only a majority of the people which did in fact approve of the Constitution. In India 'the people' enact the Constitution 'in our Constituent Assembly', but that Assembly was composed of representatives elected by a minority of the people of India and the Constitution itself was never submitted to the people directly. Is it not unreal in any case to speak of 'the people' enacting a Constitution 'in' or 'through' a constituent assembly? It is seldom indeed that the people are asked even to approve a Constitution ostensibly enacted in their name.

Moreover, once a Constitution is enacted, even when it has been submitted to the people for approval, it binds thereafter not only the institutions which it establishes, but also the people itself. They may amend the Constitution, if at all, only by the methods which the Constitution itself provides. The Constitution of the Fourth French Republic states this point well in Article 3 when it says:

National sovereignty belongs to the French people. No section of the people nor any individual may assume its exercise. The people exercise it in constitutional matters by the vote of their representatives and by the referendum. In all other matters they exercise it through their deputies in the National Assembly, elected by universal, equal, direct, and secret suffrage.

From these rather sketchy outlines of the legal basis of a Constitution's authority, it is necessary to turn now to consider the moral basis upon which a Constitution can claim authority. It was to this moral basis that William H. Seward appealed when he claimed that there is a higher law than the Constitution. We stand here upon the threshold of the great and historic debate concerning the nature and basis of political obligation and it is clear that it is quite impossible to do justice to that subject in a few pages. The most that can be attempted is to indicate the lines upon which some answers have been given to these questions which are still the subject of dispute.

If we ask what moral basis a Constitution can claim as law the answer would seem to be that it can command the authority which all law commands in a community. Whatever theory of morals may be invoked to determine and define obedience to the law will apply also to the law of the Constitution. But we may go further than this and say that there is an argument for asserting that a Constitution can command obligation on an additional ground. It is, by its nature, not just an ordinary law. It is fundamental law, it provides the basis upon which law is made and enforced. It is a prerequisite of law and order. There is indeed a moral argument for saying that a Constitution commands obedience because it is by its nature a superior or supreme law. This argument represents, in the moral field, the logical argument adopted in the legal field by Chief Justice Marshall in *Marbury* v. *Madison*. A Constitution cannot be disobeyed with the same degree of lightheartedness as a Dog Act.

It lies at the basis of political order; if it is brought into contempt, disorder and chaos may soon follow.

Just as, in the legal sphere, the logical argument for a Constitution's being supreme law was supplemented by the argument that the people, either directly or through a constituent assembly, is a supreme law-giver, so also in the moral sphere it is sometimes argued that a Constitution commands obligation because it expresses the will of the people. What the people has laid down is binding upon every individual.

Questions obviously arise when one considers the implications of these doctrines. Must we conclude that the American Constitution, for example, is binding morally upon all citizens of the United States in all circumstances, because it is a fundamental law and because it was enacted—so it declares and so the Courts declare— by the people? Abraham Lincoln went far towards asserting that it was. When he addressed himself to the seceding States in the American Civil War he said: 'A majority held in restraint by constitutional checks and limitations, and always changing easily with deliberate changes of popular opinions and sentiments, is the only true sovereign of a free people. Whoever rejects it does, of necessity, fly to anarchy or to despotism.' In his view since the people had the power to alter the Constitution, and since they were enabled freely to elect their representatives in Congress and in their State and local government, they must obey the Constitution as it was, while working hard, if they so wished, to have it amended.

Now it may be accepted that a Constitution which is capable of amendment by the people has a greater claim *prima facie* on their obedience than a Constitution which is unalterable. But consider the position within a country of a community which is in a minority, and is not only in a minority but also in a permanent minority. It can never hope to see the Constitution altered in the way it wishes nor to prevent alterations to which it is opposed. When it has exhausted all its efforts upon trying to persuade the majority to meet its demands, what is left for it? Must it acquiesce? On Lincoln's argument, the answer would be that it must. And indeed that was the answer he gave to the permanent minority of the Southern States. They must accept the Constitution, and they must not secede from the Union it established.

Because Lincoln's argument prevailed by force of arms in the American Civil War, and because the minority favoured an institution, namely slavery, which we would regard as morally indefensible, it is easy perhaps to think that Lincoln's argument is of universal validity. But can we in fact say that a permanent minority, unable to obtain what it wants under a Constitution, must continue always to obey that Constitution? The answer surely is no. There are circumstances in which it is morally right to rebel, to refuse to obey the Constitution, to upset it. A Constitution may be the foundation of law and order in a community, but mere law and order is not enough. It must be good law and good order. It is conceivable surely that a minority may be right in saying that it lives under a Constitution which establishes bad government and that, if all else is tried and fails, rebellion is right. No doubt it is difficult to say just when rebellion is right and how much rebellion is right, but that it may be legitimate is surely true.

If citizens may disobey the Constitution, may governments do so? Here, curiously enough, Abraham Lincoln used an argument which is a little inconsistent with that which he addressed to the Southern States. He held that it might be necessary for a government to disobey or neglect one part of the Constitution in order that it might save the whole. He was answering those of his critics who had condemned him for, as they alleged, suspending the right of *habeas corpus* contrary to the Constitution. Lincoln's answer was that if he had not detained certain enemies of the Union, the Union itself might have been overthrown; if he had not broken one small part of the Constitution, the whole of the rest of it would have been overthrown. 'Are all the laws but one to go unexecuted,' he said, 'and the government itself go to pieces lest that one be violated?' Here indeed we are on dangerous ground, more dangerous than that of the citizens' right to rebel. Yet it must be conceded that there are cases where a government is morally entitled, in order to save the Constitution, to break a part of it, or in order to enforce what is good in a Constitution, to neglect what is bad. Not all the articles and clauses of a Constitution, any more than all the sections of a law, are of equal value and importance. There are times when a government may have to decide what is to be saved and what lost.

These problems are often discussed as if the principal danger was that a majority may suppress the legitimate rights of a minority. It is worth while to point out that the problem arises equally under Constitutions where a majority of the people wish for a change, but a minority, by the terms of the Constitution, is able to prevent this change. This situation can arise in the United States; it can arise also in such Constitutions as those of Australia or Denmark or Switzerland. May there not be circumstances in which this majority may be morally entitled to break the Constitution?

The moral authority which a Constitution can claim may be considered, again, from the standpoint of that great school of political theory which bases its judgement of the proper extent of a government's powers upon natural law, upon the rights of man derived from natural law. Government exists to safeguard certain rights. Its actions can be justified only by the extent to which they are directed towards these ends. A Constitution can claim obedience only in so far as it establishes a government in accordance with natural law; so much of a Constitution as purports to give powers to a government beyond what is justified by natural law is void. John Locke in his *Second Treatise of Civil Government* states the case for justifiable rebellion in accordance with natural rights in classic language: 'Where the body of the people or any single man are deprived of their right, or are under the exercise of a power without right, having no appeal on earth, they have a liberty to appeal to heaven, whenever they judge the cause of sufficient moment.' And again: 'All power given with trust for the attaining an end, being limited by that end, whenever that end is manifestly neglected or opposed, the trust must necessarily be forfeited, and the power devolve into the hands of those that gave it, who may place it anew where they shall think best for their safety and security.' This view of government limited by the natural rights of man lies at the basis of the American Constitution and finds a place, as we have seen, in many modern Constitutions. It provides a moral basis upon which a government's actions can be judged and, what is more, upon which the validity of a Constitution can be tested. A Constitution binds in so far as it is in accordance with natural law. Neither a government nor a citizen may disregard the authority of a Constitution except in so far as the action can be justified by the law of nature. This is indeed 'a higher law' than a Constitution.

In the moral sphere the answer to the question 'What authority can a Constitution claim?' must be a great deal vaguer and more uncertain than in the legal sphere. To all except those moral philosophers who say that the citizen has a duty of absolute obedience to all laws always everywhere, it must be clear that there can be circumstances in which it is right for citizens and for governments to neglect or ignore or even to overthrow and suspend a Constitution. What those circumstances are will differ from place to place and from time to time. They will always be difficult to discern in practice and even more difficult to describe in theory. Some very general remarks can be made. A Constitution which is completely unalterable tends to invite and to justify disobedience. On the other hand a Constitution which is easily alterable by a numerical popular majority may so threaten or destroy the rights of a minority that it provokes the minority to justifiable disobedience, while a Constitution which permits a minority to obstruct the wishes of the majority indefinitely may lead a majority to lay violent hands upon it in just assertion of their rights. A Constitution admirably suited to the needs of its people at one time may come to be completely distorted with the passing of time and the change in the social structure of the community. Not only Constitutions themselves but the processes by which they can be changed require adaptation to changing conditions.

The moral authority which a Constitution claims and can claim is related very closely, therefore, to the structure of the community for which it purports to provide the foundations of law and order. It must embody forms of government in which a community believes; it must be adapted to their capacity for government. The mere fact that words have been inscribed upon paper can give them no special claim upon the obedience of the citizens or of the government. The whole process of so drafting a Constitution that it provides the best government of which a community is capable must be based upon the social forces operating in the community. And even when a Constitution is initiated, there begins at once to operate upon it a whole series of forces working for and against social change. What was a good Constitution may slowly be adapted into one that is better or one that is worse. It is to a consideration of these processes of change that we must now turn.

5
How Constitutions Change:
Some Primary Forces

CONSTITUTIONS, when they are framed and adopted, tend to reflect the dominant beliefs and interests, or some compromise between conflicting beliefs and interests, which are characteristic of the society at that time. Moreover they do not necessarily reflect political or legal beliefs and interests only. They may embody conclusions or compromises upon economic and social matters which the framers of the Constitution have wished to guarantee or to proclaim. A Constitution is indeed the resultant of a parallelogram of forces— political, economic, and social—which operate at the time of its adoption.

To state this is to state what is little more than a truism. Yet it is necessary to state it, if only to draw attention to the fact that if we are to understand the significance of a Constitution, we must look behind the phrase 'the people', by whom or in whose name most modern Constitutions are enacted, in order to discover what or who were the predominant forces in the framing and adoption of a Constitution. 'The people' covers a multitude of interests and opinions, many of them conflicting. In truth 'the people', 'the whole people', can be said to do very little. They never have and never could have framed a Constitution, and they never have unanimously enacted a Constitution. It was impatience with the traditional historian's habit of describing the American Constitution as the product of the people that led Dr Charles A. Beard, in 1913, to publish his essay entitled *An Economic Interpretation of the Constitution of the United States*, in which he asserted that, so far from being created by the whole people, the Constitution was the work of a consolidated group of people whose economic interests had suffered by the system of government in force under the Articles of Confederation of 1777 and who were determined to frame a Constitution which would protect and further those interests. Dr Beard investigated the property interests of the members of the Convention which drew up the Constitution; he studied their views as expressed in correspondence and debates; and he examined the extent to which the people as a whole participated in the voting which preceded the adoption of the Constitution. Here are some of the conclusions, which he states on pages 324–5 of his book:

The first firm steps towards the formation of the Constitution were taken by a small and active group of men immediately interested through their personal possessions in the outcome of their labours.

·   ·   ·   ·   ·

The members of the Philadelphia Convention which drafted the Constitution were, with a few exceptions, immediately, directly, and personally interested in, and derived economic advantages from, the establishment of the new system.

·   ·   ·   ·   ·

The Constitution was essentially an economic document based upon the concept that the fundamental private rights of property are anterior to government and morally beyond the reach of popular majorities.

·   ·   ·   ·   ·

The major portion of the members of the Convention are on record as recognizing the claim of property to a special and defensive position in the Constitution.

·   ·   ·   ·   ·

The Constitution was ratified by a vote of probably not more than one-sixth of the adult males.

When Dr Beard's book was published, his conclusions caused something of a sensation. Yet it is difficult to see why they should. The American Constitution bears clearly upon its face the marks of a belief in private property, and of a desire among its framers to protect property from certain forms of legislation which they had suffered in the past. States are forbidden to coin money, emit bills of credit, make anything but gold and silver coin legal tender, or to pass any law impairing the obligation of contracts. Private property, says Amendment V, shall not be taken for public use without just compensation. And if there were any doubt of this from the terms of the document, the supporters of the Constitution at the time dispelled it. When James Madison was writing in *The Federalist* on 23 November 1787, commending the Constitution to the people of New York, he explained that one of its virtues was that it put obstacles in the way of 'a rage for paper money, for an abolition of debts, for an equal division of property, or for any other improper or wicked project'. Indeed, as Dr Beard conceded, *The Federalist* 'presents in a relatively brief and systematic form an economic interpretation of the Constitution by the men best fitted, through an intimate knowledge of the ideals of the framers, to expound the political science of the new government'.

This is not to say that Dr Beard's book was not necessary as a timely reminder to Americans of the twentieth century of what was familiar and commonplace to Americans of the eighteenth century. It may be doubted, however, whether he has not overstated his case, whether in fact the exposition in *The Federalist* is not more judicious, revealing, and convincing, than his own elaborately documented conclusions, based upon the nature and amount of property held by the members of the Convention. What may be accepted without question is that economic interests play a part in the process of framing and adopting most Constitutions. What is more difficult to determine is the strength of those interests or forces in relation to others.

Without embarking upon intricate historical analysis, however, it is possible to see upon the face of most modern Constitutions and in the published accounts of the debates upon them, that they embody the interests and opinions of their framers or such interests and opinions as their framers think will be accepted by the body competent to adopt the Constitution. These interests and opinions cover the whole range of social life, including not only economic affairs, but also religious, national, family, or political affairs. The most obvious examples of this are, perhaps, the declarations of rights which have been inserted into Constitutions or the directive principles of social policy which found their way into the Irish and Indian Constitutions. The Constitutions of the U.S.S.R. and of the

Republics upon its frontiers all embody statements of economic and social doctrines which are in fact a manifesto of policy. At almost the other extreme is the Constitution of Eire which embodies the economic and indeed a great part of the social teaching of certain Papal Encyclicals, particularly *Rerum Novarum* (1891) and *Quadragesimo Anno* (1931). In the Constitutions of Norway and Denmark, for example, we find rights of private property asserted and safeguards for the payment of just compensation emphatically declared.

Anyone who takes the trouble to read a Constitution carefully and to consider the circumstances of its origin will accept without a shock the statement that Constitutions tend to embody or reflect or protect the social opinions of those who frame them. It has seemed necessary to discuss the point, however, because many people attach either too much or too little importance to it. This arises no doubt from the fact that to some people the economic interpretation of Constitutions—that is to say, the explanation of the extent to which the economic doctrines of their framers are recognized or safeguarded in Constitutions—is the only true and possible interpretation, while to others it is wholly false and unworthy. The matter tends to be discussed in extreme terms. Beard's analysis of the American Constitution, to which reference has just been made, provided a good example of this extremism. It was hailed by partisans as either the whole truth—which its author had never claimed it to be—or as a gross libel on the Founding Fathers. It is well, therefore, to say openly that Constitutions may well embody the social opinions of their Founders, that in some cases they may be determined predominantly by their Founders' economic opinions, and in some cases, also, be little more than an economic manifesto. But it is necessary to examine each case carefully; to submit it to analysis and to undertake fairly what in many cases will prove a most difficult and arduous study.

If it is almost a platitude that Constitutions are the product of their times, it is also true that times change. Do Constitutions change with them? How rapidly do they change, and by what processes? Does it happen often that there is grave disharmony between a Constitution and the society whose political processes it is intended to regulate? This and succeeding chapters will be devoted to a study of the relation between social change and constitutional change, to the problems which arise, to the processes by which adjustment can be made, and to the adequacy of these processes. At the outset, however, it is interesting to consider what are the forces which tend to produce constitutional change.

It is necessary to notice at the start that the forces which cause Constitutions to be changed may operate in one of two ways. First of all, they may bring about a change in circumstances which, of themselves, do not lead to any actual change in the wording of the Constitution but which cause the Constitution to mean something different from what it used to mean or which disturb its balance. The second and more obvious way in which such forces operate is that they produce circumstances which lead to a change in a Constitution either by the process of formal amendment or through judicial decision or by the growth and establishment of some custom or convention of the Constitution. A few examples may illustrate the distinction.

When the American Constitution was drafted in 1787 it gave to the Congress of the United States the power 'to regulate commerce . . . among the several states'. In those days, when the thirteen American States were sparsely populated and were primarily agricultural, there was not a great deal of 'inter-State commerce' for Congress to regulate. But with the coming in the nineteenth and twentieth centuries of those great changes which are shortly described as the industrial revolution, the commercial revolution, and, most important of all perhaps, the revolutions in the means of communication brought about by the invention of the internal combustion engine, the telephone and the telegraph, and of radio, the volume and importance of inter-State commerce increased tremendously. Without altering a single word in the Constitution the Congress of the United States acquired, through its power 'to regulate commerce . . . among the several states', authority over a wide range of activities which were of the greatest importance to the people of the United States. This authority was not taken from the States; they had never had it. It had rested from the first with the Congress, but there had not been much scope for its exercise. With the growth in inter-State commerce there came a growth in the power of the Congress of the United States and a corresponding change in the balance of power between the Union and the States which composed it. A similar change occurred in Canada and Australia also, but it has been developed to a greater degree in the United States.

It is interesting to notice some other forces which have tended to increase centralization in government by the change they make in circumstances, leaving aside for the moment any actual amendments of the Constitution which they may make necessary. War or the fear of war is a great force for centralization. In all Constitutions the defence or war power is conferred upon the central government but in times of assured peace its exercise is restricted, if not perfunctory, especially in countries under democratic government. But when rumours of war are rife and, still more, when war comes, the exercise of the defence power of the central government extends far beyond the provision of troops and munitions to the whole range of life within a community. This occurs not only in countries with unitary Constitutions but also in countries where, under a federal system, the regulation of human affairs is divided between the central and the constituent governments. In war federal governments come near to being unitary governments, not by any alteration in the words of the Constitution but by the bringing into the ambit of the defence power of many matters of great importance which in peace-time would clearly lie within the authority of the states.

Economic crisis is another great force for centralization. If the crisis arises from depression and shows itself in unemployment, or, say, from drought or floods, it is the central government alone, in a unitary or a federal system, which can place its hands upon what resources are available in the country to alleviate distress. Depressed areas need money but their governments cannot raise it; prosperous areas or less depressed areas, if there be such in a country, will not tax themselves to give donations to their poorer neighbours. It is the central government which must take money from the rich or the less poor and give it to those in need. Economic crisis in most countries usually results in the failure of local or regional or State governments to cope with their problems of unemployment assistance and in the exercise of authority in this sphere by the central government.

If the economic crisis shows itself not in unemployment and depression but in a disequilibrium in foreign trade, the central government again exercises authority, for it alone can plan the national economy and control trade with the outside world. For that matter any attempt to deal with an economic crisis involving unemployment is likely to require the intervention, in some degree, of the central government, because it alone can make plans or undertake schemes which go beyond the boundaries of local or regional authorities. These powers, in times of prosperity, may be exercised but little or not at all, and their existence is forgotten or not realized. But in time of economic crisis they are brought to life, they grow, and indeed they may come to overshadow and overbalance the whole scheme of the Constitution.

Another strong force towards centralization is the development in recent times of a series of policies known usually as 'the welfare state' or 'the social service state'. It has come to be accepted by the citizens and by the rulers of certain states, particularly of those in which universal suffrage exists, that it is the duty of governments to ensure that all citizens should be provided with a minimum standard of welfare, whether they can afford it or not. They should be provided with education, with health services, with maintenance in times of sickness or unemployment or old age. A fair share of the food that is available should be allocated to each citizen at prices which he can afford to pay. These policies have two characteristics of importance. They are expensive to carry out, for they call for a great provision of buildings and equipment and they require, for their execution, a large force of salaried workers—teachers, nurses, doctors, administrators, visitors, and inspectors—and their wages and salaries bill is consequently high. In the second place the welfare services are needed most by those who can, as a rule, afford them least. It is the rich, the healthy, the employed who must supply the funds from which the poor and the sick and the unemployed receive their assistance. Only a central government can ensure that these welfare services will be available wherever they are needed in a country. They have access to what wealth there is and they can transfer it from the better-off citizens or regions to those where the need is greater.

It is perhaps no accident that the policies of the welfare state have been developed in democracies, for they are naturally enough the policies which appeal to a majority of the people. Politicians of all parties, if they really wish to obtain power, must accept the general principles at least of the welfare state. In this respect the development of democracy is a force which has modified Constitutions, principally by increasing the power of the central government. Democracy and centralization have gone together in most countries of the world, and in many cases the connexion has been one of cause and effect. This is a predominant theme in Alexis de Tocqueville's great book, *Democracy in America*. 'It results,' he says, 'from the very constitution of democratic nations and from their necessities that the power of government among them must be more uniform, more centralized, more extensive, more searching, and more efficient than in other countries.'

Along with a strong trend towards centralization in government there has gone a trend, as these words of de Tocqueville remind us, towards the increase in the power of the executive. This change in the distribution of power in a system of government has been brought about in some cases by actual constitutional amendment, but, like the growth of centralization, it has owed a great deal to changes in circumstances which have in themselves given opportunity or scope for the executive to exercise more fully the powers which a Constitution conferred upon it. The comparison with the growth of centralization goes further. Almost all the forces which have worked for centralization, have worked also for the increase in the power of the executive. War and the fear of war, economic crisis, the policies of the 'welfare state', the growth of democracy with universal suffrage, and the demand for equality of conditions, have all produced situations in which it has been thought proper that the executive should enlarge its powers. Whether it be that the action to be taken must be swift or secret, or that the issues are complicated and uncertain, or that the execution of policies requires a band of administrators and planners and controllers, the result has always been that the executive increases in size and in power.

But other factors have strengthened the executive. The development of modern weapons of war has made it possible for a few determined men to dominate millions of unarmed citizens, if they have the nerve to do it. From the time of the invention of gunpowder up to the present, the executive, with its control over the armed forces and the police, has had its power enormously increased. The machine-gun alone is a most powerful force in the increase of the executive's control over a community. The development of radio, and of other means of communication, has strengthened the executive in other ways. Armed with a control over these powerful means of governing the citizens, the executive finds its position transformed even from the opening years of the twentieth century. There has occurred in the same period in many countries a development in the skill and efficiency of the civil service, quite apart from the increase in its numbers and in the area of its operation, which has enhanced the powers of the executive. Skill in devising improved methods of tax collection, the adoption of better methods of accounting and book-keeping, the introduction of machines into government offices—these things sound trivial, yet one by one they increase the power of executive government and enable it to exercise more effectively the authority it possesses.

Party is perhaps the most important influence upon the working of a Constitution. So important is it indeed that one is tempted to say that the Constitution is a mere skeleton; it is party which provides the flesh and blood, which gives to the body politic its life and individuality. This may be an exaggeration, but there is a great deal of truth in it. Yet few Constitutions refer specifically to party. Their framers sometimes ignored the existence of party, or thought it undesirable; in most modern Constitutions party is assumed to exist and to be essential to free government, but it is not thought necessary or desirable to recognize or regulate it in the Constitution itself. It is only in the so-called 'one-party' states that a party is given the honour of mention by name in the Constitution, as when, in Article 126 of the Constitution of the U.S.S.R. (1936) it is declared that 'the most active and politically conscious citizens from the ranks of the working class and other strata of the working people unite in the All-Union Communist Party (of Bolsheviks), which is the vanguard of the working people in their struggle to strengthen and develop the socialist system and which represents the leading nucleus of all organizations of the working people, both social and state'.

The effect which the factor of party has upon the working of a Constitution is not always easy to calculate, and it varies from country to country. In the United States, while it has clearly strengthened the executive, it provides also strength to Congress in its battles with the executive and results in the virtual paralysis of American government at certain times. In France, under the Third and Fourth Republics, the multi-party system weakened the cabinet. The Constitution endowed the executive with considerable powers, yet it could not exercise these powers with resolution or certainty because it could not count upon continuous or effective party support. Thus a set of political circumstances, outside the formal Constitution, determined the balance of power between the cabinet and the legislature in France. In some other countries of Continental Europe, however, a multi-party system does not produce such great instability of government. In Holland and Belgium and in the Scandinavian countries, parties are readier to form a coalition government with greater security of tenure than that enjoyed by most French governments. In countries in which two major parties are the contestants for power, it is common to find a cabinet in a stronger position relatively than in countries with a multi-party system. But it is not right to generalize. In each case it is necessary to analyse the structure of parties to discover how much real cohesion and unity there is behind the façade. Canada, for example, has two major parties, but the Liberal Party, though in power for many years, had to make many compromises within itself to reconcile the differences of its French-Canadian supporters with their English-speaking colleagues. A Canadian cabinet may at times exhibit the caution and compromise usually associated with coalition government.

Closely allied with party as a potent primary force in the development and modification of a Constitution is the electoral system. In some countries, as in Sweden, for example, the law regulating the electoral system is in effect a part of the Constitution; in many countries some general principles concerning the electoral system, such for example as universal suffrage or proportional representation, are prescribed or permitted by the Constitution. But in most countries the details of the electoral system, including methods of voting, the distribution of seats, the qualifications of voters, the organization of parties and the like, are regulated by ordinary law, and embodied sometimes in organic laws. These provisions are of fundamental importance in the working of a Constitution, yet they are developed and modified in many countries without any change by formal amendment in the Constitution. The system of election adopted in a country and the distribution of seats may determine the party composition of the legislature and the strength or weakness of the executive. In a great part of the United States, for example, the organization of political parties, the manner in which they may select their candidates for election (the 'primary' elections), and the qualifications which their members must possess are regulated by law which, though no part of the Constitution of the United States, has exercised an important influence upon it.

Finally, Constitutions are influenced by what people think of them, by their attitude to them. If a Constitution is regarded with veneration, if what it embodies is thought to be *prima facie* right and good, then there exists a force to preserve the Constitution against lighthearted attempts to change it. Though the formal process of amendment is there, it will be seldom and hesitatingly invoked. The Constitution of the United States occupies some such position in the eyes of the citizens. They regard it with great respect, if not with veneration. In natural reaction to this attitude, those who wish to see the Constitution amended are led to speak with exasperation of 'the Myth' of the Constitution which opposes so strong a resistance to attempts to carry through even minor reforms.

There can, indeed, be no other people anywhere in the world who regard their Constitution with greater respect than do the Americans. The Swiss alone, perhaps, can rival them. In most federal countries however there is a tendency to treat the Constitution with respect, for it is, after all, the supreme law of the land and governments are subordinate to it. Its authority is inevitably invoked from time to time against the action of legislatures and executives. In unitary States the appeal to the Constitution is not so commonly made, but it is common even there to find that the Constitution commands respect. The peoples of Holland and Belgium, or of the Scandinavian countries, see in their Constitutions a statement of some at least of those principles of good government which they believe to be important or fundamental, and they believe that government must be conducted in accordance with the Constitution. Changes, if they are to be made, should be explicit and deliberate; the Constitution must be treated with respect.

While it is true that in some countries the 'myth' of the Constitution is a strong factor for preventing or delaying change, in others the lack of anything approaching a 'myth' or even a decent respect for the Constitution leads to its being treated with contempt or indifference. If the United States represents the extreme of veneration for a Constitution, the republics of Central and South America provide many examples of the other extreme. In most cases the peoples of those republics show an attitude of ignorance or indifference to their Constitution, and the governments have little difficulty in ignoring it, amending it, or, quite frequently, in suspending it. While in these American republics it is probably true to say that the people have as little affection or respect for their government as for their Constitution, in some countries of Europe, such as the U.S.S.R. and its satellite States, it is the government which overshadows the Constitution and monopolizes the respect and awe and obedience of the citizens. There are cases, yet again, where the Constitution cannot command the respect of its citizens because it is itself a matter of controversy. In France and Italy, for example, there are parties in the State which object to the régime which the Constitution establishes and whose aim it is to establish a wholly different system. Such a situation makes reform of the Constitution difficult, because those who want reform wish to go too far, while their opponents feel it is unsafe to yield an inch. In such a case reform may be postponed for too long; it may make revolution inevitable.

This brief discussion of some of the forces or factors which bring about or affect change in Constitutions has been intended to show what a great deal of change can occur in a Constitution merely through a change in circumstances. But it will have been apparent that many of these changes in circumstances, while in themselves making a change in the nature or meaning of a Constitution, may also be instrumental in bringing about actual formal changes in the document or in leading to changes in its interpretation by judicial decision or in supplementing the Constitution by changes in Organic Law, passed by the legislature, or in forming usages or customs to supplement the formal rules of law in the Constitution. Thus, it was the demands of the economic depression of the 1930s that led the Canadians to obtain an amendment of their Constitution which, in 1940, added 'unemployment insurance' to the list of matters upon which the Parliament of Canada could legislate. The depression had already created a situation in which the government of Canada had been obliged to take the initiative in planning the economic life of the country and in giving financial assistance to the provincial governments. It had drawn the Canadian government into an extensive exercise of the powers allotted to it under the Constitution. But these powers were not enough and it was necessary therefore, in order to cope with the sort of problems which economic depressions could provide, to alter the Constitution itself by formal amendment.

The forces which have led central governments to exercise their powers more extensively have in the course of time brought to the fore the question: How is this increased activity to be paid for? In some cases central governments have found that the sources of revenue allocated to them in a Constitution are not adequate, and amendments have been secured in the Constitution to increase their capacity to acquire revenue. A good example is the Sixteenth Amendment to the Constitution of the United States, adopted in 1913, which removed from Congress certain restrictions imposed in the original Constitution upon its power to lay and collect taxes on incomes. The powers of the central government in Australia over financial matters were extended by an amendment to the Constitution adopted in 1928, and the Swiss Constitution was amended in 1915, 1919, and 1938 to give increased financial resources to the central government, particularly in order to meet defence expenditure. In Switzerland and Australia also the policies of the welfare state have led to amendments of the Constitution empowering the central government to provide these services—in Switzerland, for example, an amendment in 1925 authorized the provision of invalid, old age, and widows' pensions, and in Australia an amendment of 1946 authorized the provision of maternity allowances, widows' pensions, child-endowment, unemployment, pharmaceutical, sickness, and hospital benefits, medical and dental services, benefits to students, and family allowances.

But these forces which change Constitutions do not lead necessarily to actual formal amendment. They produce a change in circumstances which may lead to a dispute about whether in fact the powers of a government under a Constitution are sufficient to justify it in acting to deal with these circumstances. Here the case of the 'commerce power' of Congress in the Constitution of the United States provides a good example. It was pointed out earlier in this chapter that the great increase in the extent and in the intensity of commerce between the States as a result of the industrial and commercial revolutions and the revolutions in communications, had of itself increased the opportunities of the government of the United States to exercise its powers. But with this admitted increase, there arose disputes about the limits of power and the Supreme Court of the United States was called upon to decide from time to time whether a given matter did or did not lie within the power of Congress to regulate commerce 'among the states'. The modern economic system of the United States, produced by these revolutionary movements which have been mentioned, was unlike anything that the framers of the Constitution had conceived. Was it indeed possible nowadays to make the distinction between inter-State commerce and intra-State commerce which they appeared to envisage? Could you draw a line, and where should it be drawn? The Supreme Court almost from its inception has been obliged to consider this question. In modern times, it was called upon to decide whether the National Industrial Recovery Act, passed by Congress in 1933 as part of President Franklin D. Roosevelt's 'New Deal', was valid or not. It admitted the difficulty of the question but it gave an answer, declaring the Act invalid (*Schechter Poultry Corp.* v. *United States* 295 U.S. 495).

The powers of a central government in war provide a similar example. Obviously a state of war gives an opportunity for a government to exercise to the full powers which in peace lie dormant and in so doing it becomes a stronger government. But disputes may still arise about the limits of the defence power. Courts, in federal countries particularly, are called upon to settle these questions and a whole series of decisions have been given in Australia and Canada particularly on this question. Economic depression similarly intensifies action by the central government, but it may also raise questions of the extent of its powers. In Canada in the 1930s a series of measures was passed by Mr. Bennett's government to meet some of the problems raised by the economic depression, and they were challenged in the courts on the ground that they went beyond the powers granted to the parliament of Canada. Almost all these measures were declared invalid by the Judicial Committee of the Privy Council in 1937 (*Attorney-General of Canada* v. *Attorney-General of Ontario*, [1937] A.C. 326 and 355).

Some of the factors which lead to constitutional change show themselves not so much in bringing about formal amendments to the Constitution nor in providing situations from which disputes arise concerning jurisdiction which must be decided by a court, but rather in leading to the establishment of certain understandings or practices or customs which are not rules of law but which influence the working of the rules of law embodied in the Constitution. A more detailed discussion of this process will be given in Chapter 8 but it will be useful to illustrate the point here by one example. It has been mentioned already that party organization affects the balance of powers in a Constitution, particularly in regard to the strength of the executive as against the legislature. But party can go further and actually establish certain rules of government whose sanction is chiefly to be found in party discipline. Thus in the United States the fact that the President is in practice elected directly by the people voting in their States and not indirectly through Colleges of Electors as the Constitution prescribes, is a result of party organization. The candidates for the presidency are party candidates and the members of the Electoral Colleges are party men pledged to support the party's candidate. This is so well understood that it can be regarded as a rule, an established custom or convention of the American system of government. It does not produce a formal amendment of the Constitution; it does not actually contradict the law of the Constitution. It supplements it and modifies it; it produces a change in its working.

In the three chapters which follow, some discussion is undertaken of the way in which Constitutions change as a result of the operation of the sort of forces which have been discussed in this chapter. This discussion proceeds upon the understanding that many important changes in the working of a Constitution occur without any alterations in the rules which regulate a government, whether they be strictly legal or rules of custom and convention. This lies in the background or at the basis of any discussion of constitutional change. It is often difficult to describe and assess, particularly because it is seldom stationary. Upon this basis we discuss, one by one, the ways in which Constitutions are changed through the exercise of the process of formal amendment, through the exercise of the process of judicial decision, and finally by the formation of usages and conventions. Each of these three processes reacts upon, modifies, supplements, and occasionally nullifies the other. They are separable for the purposes of exposition, but they operate together in the day-to-day working of a Constitution. They vary in their relative importance from time to time and from place to place. Upon their effective co-operation the health and flexibility, the growth and strength of a Constitution depends.

6
How Constitutions Change:
Formal Amendment

WHEN THE CLASSIFICATION of Constitutions was discussed in an earlier chapter, reference was made to the distinction between Constitutions which could be amended by the ordinary legislative process and those for whose amendment some special process was required—a distinction commonly described as one between flexible and rigid Constitutions. Most modern Constitutions are 'rigid' in this sense; very few—New Zealand is one example—can be altered by the ordinary legislative process. There is a great variety in the amending processes prescribed in Constitutions and it is not easy to find any common principles behind them. But it seems possible to make one or two generalizations from the study of these provisions about the objects which the amending process appears to be intended to secure or safeguard.

Speaking generally it would seem that the amending process in most modern Constitutions is aimed at safeguarding one or more of four objectives. The first is that the Constitution should be changed only with deliberation, and not lightly or wantonly; the second is that the people should be given an opportunity of expressing their views before a change is made; the third is that, in a federal system, the powers of the units and of the central government should not be alterable by either party acting alone; and the fourth is that individual or community rights—for example, of minorities in language or religion or culture—should be safeguarded. In some Constitutions one only of these considerations has operated; in others two or three or all four have had an effect. There can be few 'rigid'

Constitutions whose amending process cannot be explained substantially by one or more of these four considerations. Of the first of these four—deliberation—little need be said. The Constitution lies behind government and should be treated with respect. But of the other three rather more must be said.

In many, if not most, modern Constitutions it is thought proper that the people or the electorate should have some say in deciding whether an amendment should be made or not. This is an illustration, in the case of the amending process, of that general doctrine of the sovereignty of the people and of the power of the people to enact and give to themselves a Constitution, which has been discussed already in Chapter 4. It follows logically from that doctrine. The people's will is discovered in a variety of ways. Sometimes the proposed amendment is actually referred to the people after it has been passed by the legislature. This is the procedure required, for example, by the Constitution of the Republic of Ireland, of Denmark, of the Commonwealth of Australia, and of Switzerland, and by the Constitution of each of the fifty American States.

The will of the people may be sought in a different way. The legislature itself may be given power to make the amendment, but it may be required to delay its final action until a general election has been held, thus ensuring that the people may, if they choose, express their views upon the proposal in voting for candidates at the election. In Belgium, when a proposal to amend the Constitution is brought forward, both houses of the legislature must be dissolved and after re-election the amendment must be passed by a two-thirds majority in each house at a session at which at least two-thirds of the members are present before it can become effective. In Denmark, before the proposed amendment is submitted to a referendum of the people, as mentioned above, it must have been approved in both houses of the legislature before and after a general election. In Holland also there must be a general election of both houses and thereafter the amendment must be passed by a two-thirds majority in both houses. Sweden requires a majority vote in each house of the Riksdag before and after a general election while in Norway there is added the further safeguard that the approval of a two-thirds majority of the Storting is necessary after the general election. In

Colombia and Ecuador an amendment must be approved by a majority in each house in two successive Congresses.

In some countries a reference to the people may occur but need not. Thus in France under the Constitution of the Fifth Republic an amendment must be submitted to a referendum unless it has been carried by a three-fifths majority in a joint sitting of both houses— the Senate and the National Assembly. By the Italian Constitution of 1948, a proposed amendment approved by the legislature must be submitted to a referendum if within three months one-fifth of the members of the lower house or 500,000 voters or five regional councils so request, unless the proposal was carried by a two-thirds majority in each house. In Chile by the Constitution of 1925 an amendment must obtain first a majority in each house sitting separately and then a majority in both houses sitting together and with a majority of its total membership present, but it may thereafter in certain circumstances be referred to a popular vote by the president.

In the examples that have been quoted so far, the share of the people in the process of amending the Constitution is confined to approval or disapproval of a proposal initiated by the legislature. But in some countries it is thought proper that an opportunity should be given to the people to take the initiative themselves and put forward proposals for constitutional amendment. Switzerland is the home of this practice which is called 'the initiative'. There is a variety of ways in which the initiative can operate in Switzerland to amend the Constitution. If 50,000 qualified voters demand it, the question of the total revision of the Constitution must be referred to the vote of the Swiss people, and if a majority approves, the two houses of the legislature (the Federal Assembly) are then dissolved and after the general elections proceed to a general revision which, in its turn, must be submitted to a referendum of the people. On the other hand, it is open to 50,000 voters to initiate not a proposal for a general revision of the Constitution but a proposal for a specific amendment either in general terms or in the form of an actual draft. If the proposal is made in general terms, the Federal Assembly, if it approves of the proposal, produces a draft and it is submitted for the approval of the people. If the Federal Assembly does not approve of the proposal, the people are asked to decide whether they wish for an amendment in the general terms proposed, and if they agree, the Federal Assembly must draft the amendment. If the proposal, on the other hand, is put forward as an actual draft by the 50,000 voters, and the Federal Assembly approves it, it is submitted forthwith to the people; if the Federal Assembly does not approve, it may submit a counter-proposal to the people who will decide between the two proposals.

In thirteen of the fifty States in the American Union there is provision for constitutional amendment by means of the initiative. The requirements differ in detail from State to State, but in general the rule is that when a certain percentage of qualified voters—varying from 8 per cent to 15 per cent—demand it, a proposal to amend the Constitution must be submitted to the electorate.

When the machinery for amending a federal Constitution comes to be considered a new factor must be taken into account. The principle of a federal government is that powers are divided between a government for the whole country and governments for its parts, and that these governments are independent of each other within their own spheres. It follows from this that the amending process must be so devised that neither the central government acting alone nor the constituent governments alone can alter the division of power in the Constitution. It is usually considered best that some form of amendment which involves joint action by the central government and the constituent governments should be adopted. This is the position in the United States where amendment of the Constitution may be made if the proposal is passed by a two-thirds majority in each house of Congress, and is thereafter accepted by a vote of the legislatures of three-quarters of the States. A similar provision is found in the Constitution of India, so far as amendment of the division of powers is concerned, though the consent of the legislatures of one half of the States will suffice.

In some federal systems the principle that the people should be associated directly with the process of constitutional amendment is linked with the requirements of a federal system and it is provided that an amendment, after passing through the two houses of the central legislature, must be submitted to a referendum of the people and that only if it is accepted not merely by a majority of all the electors voting but also by a majority of electors voting in a majority of the constituent units of the federation, may the amendment be carried. This is the rule in Switzerland and Australia. They recognize the necessities of federation by ensuring that no change in the Constitution may be carried out by the central legislature or the regional legislatures acting alone; at the same time they assert that the relations between these two sets of governments are not matters for the governments alone—as might perhaps be inferred from the American process of amendment—but are matters for the people, acting in their dual capacity of citizens of the whole country and citizens of the constituent parts. In a unitary State it may be enough to say that a majority of all the electors voting in a referendum is sufficient to carry an amendment; in a federal State something more is needed—the people as citizens of the units must express their views.

There need be no uniformity about the amending process in a federal country. So far as the federal principle is concerned, as long as the powers of constitutional amendment are not confided exclusively to the central government alone or to the constituent governments alone, any arrangement is consistent with the requirements of federalism. In Canada until 1950 neither central nor provincial governments, alone or in co-operation, could amend the Constitution—that power rested only with the parliament of the United Kingdom. That was the extreme position. But it is interesting to notice that the requirements, as many conceive them, of popular sovereignty, of requiring the consent of the people to constitutional amendment, can be combined with the requirements of federalism, as is done in Australia and Switzerland.

When the safeguarding of rights is attempted, whether of individuals or minorities, a variety of devices is adopted in accordance with the circumstances. Here the Constitution of Switzerland provides once more some interesting examples. The method of altering the Swiss Constitution safeguards not only the sovereignty of the people and the federal principle, but also certain individual and community rights. Thus it is declared in the Constitution that German, French, and Italian are the three official languages of the federation and that these three along with Romansch make up the four national languages. These provisions are thus placed above the level of ordinary law; they have constitutional guarantees; they cannot be altered except by the special process of constitutional amendment. A similar protection is given in the Canadian Constitution to the status of the French and English languages. 'Either the English or the French language may be used,' the Constitution states, 'by any person in the debates of the Houses of Parliament of Canada and of the Houses of the Legislature of Quebec and both these languages shall be used in the respective records and journals of these Houses; and either of these languages may be used by any person or in any pleading or process in or issuing from any court of Canada established under this Act, and in or from all or any of the courts of Quebec. The Acts of the Parliament of Canada and of the Legislature of Quebec shall be printed and published in both these languages.'

In a federal Constitution the safeguarding of minority rights tends to be accomplished by the same restrictions upon the process of constitutional amendment as is the safeguarding of the federal nature of the Constitution itself, and this is not surprising because it often happens—and the French-Canadians of Quebec provide a good example—that it is the existence of minority communities that accounts in large measure for the country's choosing a federal rather than a unitary government. But the two points may be distinguished and indeed they were distinguished in Canada when, in 1950, discussions began on the question of devising a process of constitutional amendment to replace that hitherto existing by which the Constitution could be amended only by an act of the parliament of the United Kingdom. There was general agreement among the representatives of the provinces and of Canada that the safeguards needed to protect the minority rights of language and religion must be more rigid and absolute than those to protect the division of powers between the central and provincial legislatures.

When the Constitution of the Union of South Africa was being drafted in 1909 safeguards were sought for the position of the English and Dutch languages. When it was decided that the Constitution should be unitary and not federal, it was necessary to provide a special procedure for the amendment of that part of the Constitution which guaranteed these and other community rights, and it was laid down accordingly that such portions of the Constitution might be amended only by a two-thirds majority of the total number of members of both houses of the Union parliament at a joint sitting of those houses. This safeguard was an effective legal check so long as the Constitution of the Union, as an act of the British parliament, had supremacy over legislation by the Union parliament. With the passing of the Statute of Westminster, 1931, and the conferring upon the parliament of the Union of the power to amend acts of the British parliament, it was held that the safeguard continued to be effective in law.

It is natural to ask now how these various methods of altering Constitutions, devised to secure and safeguard the objects which have been described above in a general sort of way, have worked in practice. Are Constitutions frequently amended? Are they amended too seldom or too often? Are most Constitutions considered satisfactory by those who live under them? It must be confessed that it is very difficult to answer this question in any general way because so few Constitutions in existence today have had a long enough history upon which to base any opinion. Of the Constitutions in force in Europe in the middle of the twentieth century, only those of Sweden (1809), Norway (1814), Holland (1815), Belgium (1831), and Switzerland (1848) were in force before 1914. (The modern Constitution of Denmark, based on that of 1863, came into operation in 1920.) If to these we add the Constitution of the United States (1787), the Constitutions of a few members of the British Commonwealth—Canada (1867), New Zealand (1852), Australia (1901), South Africa (1909)—and the Constitutions of one or two Latin-American Republics, we have the total of the countries which can provide us with anything like forty years or more of continuous history under a Constitution and of the experience of attempting to adapt that Constitution by an amending process.

It is worth while perhaps to emphasize the way in which Constitutions have come and gone in the first half of the twentieth century. Two World Wars provided the occasion for many of these changes. By the end of the First World War the Constitutions of Imperial Germany, of Imperial Russia, of the Austro-Hungarian Empire, and of the Turkish Empire, had been overwhelmed. In the next few years there arose new Constitutions, often for new States set up in the ruins of old Empires. There were new Constitutions for Germany (the so-called 'Weimar' Constitution of 1919), the

D

U.S.S.R. (1924 and 1936), Poland (1921), Czechoslovakia (1920), Jugoslavia (1921), Austria (1921), Hungary (1920), Estonia (1920), Lithuania (1928), Latvia (1922), Greece (1927), Roumania (1923), Albania (1925), Finland (1919), Portugal (1933), and Spain (1931). By the end of the Second World War most of these Constitutions had ceased to operate and had been joined in destruction by the older, pre-1914 Constitutions of France and Italy; in Finland, Portugal, and the U.S.S.R. alone, perhaps, could it be claimed that the Constitution still preserved some semblance of its former self. In the years after 1945 new Constitutions began once more to appear, but in smaller numbers and with less liberal and democratic exuberance than in the years after 1918. There were new Constitutions for France (1946 and 1958), Italy (1948), the Federal Republic of Western Germany (1948), the Federal People's Republic of Jugoslavia (1946), Burma (1947), Ceylon (1948), India (1950), while in Austria and in Czechoslovakia an attempt was made to revive the old Constitutions of 1920 with some modifications, an attempt which was to fail in Czechoslovakia with the Communist *coup* of 1948 and the subsequent adoption of a new Constitution for a 'people's democratic republic'.

It is apparent from this account of the rise and fall of Constitutions that in Europe there are few countries which provide a sufficiently long and stable period of experience under a Constitution to enable one to consider, with any profit, the way in which the process of formal constitutional amendment has worked and how effective it has been. The Constitutions of most European countries have in fact not had a fair trial; they have not been given a chance to show whether they could work or not.

The same situation is found, broadly speaking, in Central and South America. In few of the republics has there occurred even twenty years' continuous government in accordance with the terms of a Constitution, and in some cases one Constitution has followed another in quick succession and in equal ineffectiveness. Between 1933 and 1948 fourteen new Constitutions were adopted in Latin America, and of these Brazil supplied three, one each in 1934, 1937, and 1946. It is true that in many cases these new Constitutions reproduce a good deal that was found in their predecessors, but in practice the frequency with which Constitutions come and go in most

Latin-American States makes any study of their ordered development impossible.

From what has been said so far, it will be seen that any study of the working of the amending process in Constitutions must be confined to a few countries in Europe and in the British Commonwealth, and to the Constitution of the United States. If we ask the question in relation to these countries: Are Constitutions frequently amended? the answer appears to be that, with few exceptions, they are not. It is interesting to consider why this should be.

If we look first at unitary Constitutions, we realize that one great source of proposals for amendment—the alteration of the division of powers—is absent. The degree of decentralization or of centralization in a unitary State is a matter which can be regulated by ordinary law. What matters remain, then, which are likely to give rise to demands for amendment? In the first fifty years of the twentieth century, there appear to have been two main issues only—the right to vote, and the method of voting. Constitutions have been amended from time to time to widen the franchise, introducing manhood suffrage or, later on, womanhood suffrage. Thus the Swedish Constitution was amended in 1909 to permit manhood suffrage and in 1921 to permit womanhood suffrage; in Norway manhood suffrage was finally established in 1913 after a series of amendments, and votes were granted to women on a limited scale in 1907 and on equal terms with men in 1913. In 1915 a thorough revision of the Danish Constitution of 1863 had as its main object the grant of the vote to all citizens over the age of twenty-five and the introduction of a wider franchise in the process of selecting members of the upper house of the legislature. In these same three Scandinavian countries, the Constitutions were amended to permit the introduction of systems of proportional representation, in Sweden in 1909, in Norway in 1913, and in Denmark in 1915. In Holland and Belgium similar changes were made. The franchise was extended in Holland by constitutional amendments in 1917 and 1922 and in Belgium in 1920 and 1921, and proportional representation was provided for in Holland in 1917 and in Belgium in 1893.

If we turn now to the experience of the use of the amending process in relation to federal Constitutions—and in particular those of the United States, Canada, Australia, and Switzerland—it is interesting to see how communities vary in their willingness to undertake amendment. The four countries mentioned have had a continuous history under the Constitution which is at present in force and they provide material upon which one can form some conclusions. The Constitution of the United States, which was adopted in 1789, had been formally amended on twenty-two occasions up to 1960. The first ten of these amendments, however, were adopted in 1791 and in effect were part of the original Constitution. In the one hundred and fifty years and more which elapsed since 1791, then, the American Constitution had been amended only twelve times. Swiss experience provides an interesting contrast. Although the Swiss Constitution of 1848 was amended only eleven times in the first fifty years of its operation, it was amended thirty-seven times in its second half-century. In Australia the method of altering the Constitution is similar to that in Switzerland—it requires not only the approval of the legislature but also of a majority of all the electors voting in a referendum and also a majority of electors in a majority of the States in the federation. In the sixty years in which the Australian Constitution has been in force, it has been amended four times only. Finally the Canadian Constitution of 1867, whose amendment could be carried out, up to 1950, by the parliament of the United Kingdom only, was amended in that period at least fourteen times—though there is room for argument that even more amendments may have occurred.

What conclusions can be drawn from the experience of these four countries? Is the process of formal amendment too difficult? Are there too many hurdles to clear? It has been maintained frequently that to require, as in Australia and Switzerland, the reference of an amendment to the people, and particularly to the people in two capacities, is to place excessive restrictions upon the amending process. It is argued that the people are likely, through ignorance or indifference or distrust of government, to vote against proposals for constitutional amendment. The experience of Australia seems to support this argument. The Constitution has been amended on four occasions only, but twenty-three proposals for amendment had been placed before the people on eleven separate occasions up to 1960. It is important to remark, however, that in all these cases except three the proposal was rejected not only because it failed to obtain the support of a majority of electors in a majority of the States, but also because it failed to obtain a majority of all the electors voting. In three cases only, therefore, could it be said that the extra safeguard imposed by the Constitution had come into operation to prevent what a majority of the people wanted. None the less it is apparent that the people of Australia have shown a conservative attitude towards the amendment of their Constitution.

But when we consider Swiss experience it is apparent that the people are not conservative everywhere. In the hundred years from 1848 ninety-six proposals for amending the Constitution were submitted to the people and of these forty-eight were accepted. More significant perhaps is the fact that since 1874, when the Constitution was submitted to a general revision, the legislature has submitted forty-one proposals for constitutional amendment to the people and thirty-four of these were accepted. The people have been much less ready to accept proposals put forward on the initiative of 50,000 voters—only seven out of thirty-five such proposals were accepted. What is apparent, however, is that if the Swiss legislature is in favour of constitutional amendment, it has seldom been obstructed by the people, in spite of the considerable obstacles that must be overcome to obtain approval for an amendment. It would seem that, although the procedure for amendment may be extremely rigid, the ease with which it may be worked will depend upon the outlook of the people. It comes as something of a surprise to find that in this matter the Swiss, so often regarded as a conservative people, should be readier to accept proposals for change than the radical Australians.

A glance at the experience of the States in the American Union appears to show that a requirement that the people must approve of constitutional amendment—a requirement that is found, in one form or another, in all the fifty Constitutions—does not necessarily make actual amendment infrequent. While the State of Tennessee had not changed its Constitution at all in the eighty years after its adoption in 1870, and the Constitutions of Illinois (1870) and Kentucky (1891) had been amended in only a few particulars, the Constitutions of South Carolina, California, Georgia, and Louisiana had all received more than one hundred amendments. Evidently people vary from State to State in their attitude to constitutional change.

When we try to form a conclusion about the suitability of the formal amending process in modern Constitutions, it is clear that no valid generalization can be offered. It is possible to produce examples where an amendment has been rejected by a very small margin and where it seems ridiculous that such great obstacles should be put in the way of change. The experience of Denmark is perhaps a classic example. In 1939 proposals to amend the Constitution, which had passed both houses of the Riksdag before and after a general election, as the Constitution (amended in 1915) required, were submitted to the people for approval. The Constitution requires that an amendment to be carried must obtain the support not only of a majority of all the electors voting, but also of at least 45 per cent of those entitled to vote. On this occasion, although the proposals received the support of a majority of those voting, they obtained the support of only 44·46 per cent of the qualified voters.

This was an extreme case, and indeed it is easier to imagine such extreme cases than to encounter them. Thus it is frequently pointed out that, under the provisions for amendment of the Constitution of the United States whereby a proposed amendment must after being approved by a two-thirds majority in each House of Congress be accepted by the legislatures of three-quarters of the States, that thirteen States with a combined population less than that of the single State of New York can prevent the remaining thirty-seven States from achieving their will—that one-tenth of the population can obstruct nine-tenths. In fact there have been no such cases. Whenever Congress has put forward a proposal for amendment, it has usually been accepted—twenty-two amendments have been carried out of twenty-seven proposed by Congress. And once proposed they have been accepted fairly quickly. Six amendments came into effect in the twenty years from 1913 to 1933—the first, removing some restrictions on the powers of Congress to levy income tax, was proposed by Congress in 1909 and proclaimed in 1913; the second, providing for the direct election of senators in place of their indirect election by State legislatures, was proposed in 1912 and proclaimed in 1913; the third, imposing prohibition, was proposed in 1917 and proclaimed in 1919; the fourth, granting votes to women, was proposed in 1919 and proclaimed in 1920; the fifth, adjusting the terms of office of the President and Vice-President and of Congress, was proposed in 1932 and proclaimed in 1933; and the sixth, repealing the prohibition amendment of 1919, was proposed in February 1933 and proclaimed in November 1933. On the other hand, the amendment limiting the number of terms for which a president might hold office took more than four years to be ratified. It was proposed in January 1947 and adopted in February 1951. Needless to say there had been a long period of agitation before some of these amendments were carried through Congress, but once this was achieved the assent of sufficient State legislatures was usually obtained and obtained speedily.

It is sometimes asked whether, had the process of amending the American Constitution been easier, the Civil War of 1861-5 might have been avoided. From time to time in the years that preceded the outbreak of the war, attempts were made to introduce amendments to the Constitution which might satisfy the North and South, but none of these proposals obtained sufficient support. It is true that the veto which a few Southern States could exercise through their senators upon the North's proposals for amendment roused the Northerners to exasperation and frustration and fury; it is true also that as the South saw more and more free States established in the Union they realized that their veto would wither away and they became desperate and driven to consider secession. But had the process of amendment been simpler, had the North been entitled to have its way by a simple majority, had, in short, a majority of the people of the United States been entitled to prevail over a minority in amending the Constitution, the secession of the South would most certainly have occurred as soon as any such amendment had been carried. The amending process may have focused the differences between North and South upon the Constitution but it did not create those differences or exacerbate them. It was only after Civil War had been tried and the North had been victorious that it was possible to amend the Constitution in terms which the North approved. Indeed it may be said that the amending process in the American Constitution suits admirably the divisions of opinion and the attitude towards government of the people of the United States. If they are clear that they want a change, they can get it speedily. If they are doubtful and divided, they must proceed slowly—and they should.

The question that has just been discussed in relation to the American Constitution may be considered also in relation to those Constitutions of Europe and of the rest of the world which have been overthrown or disregarded. Would an easier amending process or a more frequent use of the amending process have given them a longer life? Could they have been successfully adapted to meet changing conditions? In many cases the failure or overthrow of these Constitutions was the result of forces which would not have been capable of expression through an amending process. Defeat in war was responsible for the disappearance of many of them. In other cases a revolutionary movement, designed to overthrow the existing régime embodied in the Constitution, prevailed as the result either of war or of insurrection and overturned the Constitution. Even the simplest and easiest forms of constitutional amendment are irrelevant to revolutionary movements of this kind. Revolutions are often brought about by a minority which could never have achieved its end through the process of constitutional amendment. Then again Constitutions are sometimes suspended or overthrown by governments which regard them with contempt and do not trouble to amend them. They could amend them if they chose, but they prefer to gain their ends by more direct means. Most of the cases in the first half of the twentieth century where Constitutions have passed out of existence fell into these categories.

One of the most interesting examples to consider perhaps is the Constitution of the Third French Republic. It was always a controversial document. It did not command the loyalty of all the citizens. Yet it proved remarkably durable and survived from 1875 to 1940. In those sixty-five years only three formal amendments were made to the Constitution; one in 1879 to permit the moving of the seat of government from Versailles to Paris; another in 1884 when provisions were inserted that the republican form of government should not be made the subject of a proposed amendment and that members of families that had reigned in France should be ineligible for the presidency of the Republic; and one in 1926 whereby M. Poincaré's financial policies were given the support of a constitutional guarantee from a sinking fund. Here was a Constitution that, superficially at any rate, seemed to satisfy people, yet upon the defeat of 1940 it went virtually into abeyance and in the victory of 1945 it was thought best to make a fresh start with a newly drafted document. Yet it would not be right to conclude that if the French Constitution had been amended more frequently it might have survived longer. The process of amendment was not complicated—all that was required for an amendment to be carried was a simple majority in a joint sitting of both houses at Versailles. The cure for French political ills could not be found in the amendment of constitutional provisions. The political structure of the country, its party system, its deep divisions of opinion, produced its instability of government. Yet it is reasonable to prophesy that had France not been defeated in 1940, the Constitution of 1875 would have survived, perhaps without further amendment. The fact that the Constitution of the Fourth Republic resembled that of the Third Republic in so many respects is evidence that the old compromises had a certain value.

It may be concluded that, for the most part, countries which have taken their Constitutions seriously have been able to make sufficient use of their process of formal amendment to justify us in saying that the process is not unduly rigid or cumbersome. It must be recognized and emphasized also that there are some political ills or political controversies which cannot be dealt with satisfactorily by any process of constitutional amendment, no matter how simple or 'flexible'. At the same time it is worth while to remark that there are criticisms which may legitimately be made of the amending process in some countries. Quite apart from examples of unduly rigid requirements like that already quoted from Denmark, there exists in many Constitutions an unnecessary uniformity in the amending process. In some Constitutions any change of any kind in any part of the Constitution can only be made by the one, uniform amending process. This process may have been devised originally to safeguard a particular part of the Constitution but it is extended in its scope to the whole Constitution. This is unnecessary. It would be perfectly proper to say that some parts of a Constitution may be altered by a simple majority of the legislature, that other parts may be altered only with the approval of the people; that some parts of a federal Constitution, for example, may be altered with the consent of the people or the legislatures of a majority of the States and others only with the unanimous consent of all the States. It is true that in some Constitutions there is variety of this kind, but in many there is a uniformity which imposes quite unnecessary restrictions upon the amendment of parts of a Constitution.

In this respect the Constitution of India strikes a good balance. It places extra safeguards in the amending process so far as those parts of the Constitution are concerned which contain the division of powers between the States and the Union, and it requires the concurrence of the legislatures of at least half the States in their amendment. The amendment of the rest of the Constitution, however, may be carried out by the legislature, provided it receives the approval of an absolute majority of the membership of each house and a two-thirds majority of those present and voting. In some Constitutions also there are found provisions which are to continue in operation until the legislature otherwise provides, thus making a part of the Constitution subject to a different amending process. This variety in the amending process is wise, but it is rarely found.

It must be admitted, too, that the safeguards which are embodied in the amending process in many Constitutions can be abused. Constitutions become antiquated and cumbersome because the effort required to alter them is too great. In some State Constitutions in the American Union this is admitted to be so. A practice which might well be regarded as an abuse, too, is that of inserting into Constitutions articles and amendments which are not truly constitutional in character. In this way policies are given a protection greater than that which the ordinary law provides. This practice is most common perhaps in the United States, and has led to State Constitutions becoming lengthy, ill-arranged, and heterogeneous. Worse still they restrict the operation of the legislature and executive in matters which properly belong to them—salaries of officials, the law of property, the conditions of labour, the borrowing of money, the organization of the judiciary, of school boards, and so on. Yet it would be difficult to persuade a majority of the citizens of these States that they should deny themselves this power to make some laws fundamental and superior to others. The American's distrust of government leads him to favour the rigid amending process which his Constitution gives him and to extend its use to other than strictly constitutional matters.

It may be said in general, however, that where communities have lived under constitutional government, where, that is to say, the Constitution has been in effective operation and where it has been regarded with respect, the process of formal amendment has seldom proved too difficult for the necessary adaptation of the Constitution to any strongly felt needs in the community. When a Constitution has been suspended or destroyed it would be difficult to say that a too rigid amending process had contributed to its disappearance. But it may be emphasized that one reason why the process of formal amendment has proved adequate in most Constitutions is that it does not operate alone. There are other processes at work in modifying a Constitution and we have now to consider one of the most important of them—judicial interpretation.

7

How Constitutions Change: Judicial Interpretation

IT IS NATURAL to ask at the outset of this chapter how it comes about that Courts and judges come to perform the function of interpreting a Constitution. The answer may be stated shortly in this way. It is the function of judges to decide what the law is, in disputed cases. A Constitution is part of the law and it therefore falls within the purview of the judges. Moreover it may happen that there appears to be some conflict between the law of the Constitution and some other rule of law or some action, whether of the legislature or of the executive. If the judges are to decide what the law is in such a case, they must determine the meaning not only of the rule of ordinary law but also of the law of the Constitution. And if, in terms, a Constitution imposes restrictions upon the powers of the institutions it sets up, then the Courts must decide whether their actions transgress those restrictions, and in doing so, the judges must say what the Constitution means.

The logical justification for judicial interpretation of a Constitution finds its most concise expression in the words which Chief Justice Marshall used when, in 1803, the Supreme Court of the United States, in the case of *Marbury* v. *Madison* (1 Cranch 137), first declared an act of Congress void. 'It is emphatically the province and duty of the judicial department to say what the law is,' he said. 'Those who apply the rule to particular cases, must of necessity expound and interpret that rule. If two laws conflict with each other, the Courts must decide on the operation of each. So if a law be in opposition to the Constitution; if both the law and the

Constitution apply to a particular case, so that the Court must either decide that case conformably to the law, disregarding the Constitution, or conformably to the Constitution, disregarding the law, the Court must determine which of these conflicting rules governs the case. This is of the very essence of judicial duty. If, then, the Courts are to regard the Constitution, and the Constitution is superior to any ordinary act of the legislature, the Constitution, and not such ordinary act, must govern the case to which they both apply.'

The substance of the matter is that while it is the duty of every institution established under the authority of a Constitution and exercising powers granted by a Constitution, to keep within the limits of those powers, it is the duty of the Courts, from the nature of their function, to say what these limits are. And that is why Courts come to interpret a Constitution.

In some Constitutions this duty of the Courts is explicitly recognized. Thus in the Constitution of the Republic of Ireland, it is provided that the jurisdiction of the High Court, and, on appeal, of the Supreme Court, shall extend to the question of the validity of any law having regard to the provisions of the Constitution (Art. 34). In some cases the power of the Courts to interpret the Constitution is inferred from the Constitution or from the nature of the judicial function. This appears to be the position in the United States and the words of Chief Justice Marshall quoted above were the first and authoritative statement of the Supreme Court's assumption of that power. In most countries where the Anglo-American view of the law prevails or has exercised some influence it is accepted that the Courts have jurisdiction to interpret the Constitution and if necessary to declare acts passed by the legislature to be void on the ground that they conflict with the Constitution. Judicial review is found, for example, in Australia and its six states, in all fifty States of the American Union, in Canada and its ten provinces, in India, and in the Republics of Central and South America. Among European countries, it prevails in the cantons, but not in the federal government of Switzerland; and it was embodied in the Austrian Constitution of 1920, in the Italian Constitution of 1948, and, in a sense, in the Constitution of the Fifth French Republic.

This function of the Courts will vary in extent according to the terms of the Constitution. If a Constitution imposes many restrictions upon a government and in particular upon a legislature, then the opportunities to seek a Court's interpretation will be all the greater. As a general rule a Court does not take the initiative in these matters. It interprets a Constitution only when, in the course of proceedings before it upon a case, a question arises concerning the meaning of the Constitution. In some countries, like France, Eire, India, and Canada, the law provides that a bill or an act of the legislature or some question of law may be referred to a Court by the executive for a judgement upon its validity, in the light of the provisions of the Constitution. When this is done the validity of a law can be decided without waiting for a case to arrive, and any uncertainty about its validity can be removed. But here again it will be noted that it is not the Court which takes the initiative.

It must not be supposed however that Courts in all countries exercise the power to interpret a Constitution and incidentally to annul acts of the legislature. Sometimes the Constitution expressly excludes a part, at any rate, of its provisions from their jurisdiction. In the Constitutions of Ireland and of India, for example, it is provided that no Court may take cognizance of the extent to which laws made by the parliament are in accordance with the declarations of the principles of social policy which are enshrined in these Constitutions. In the Constitution of Switzerland it is laid down (Art. 113) that while the Federal Tribunal may declare cantonal laws invalid, it must apply without question the laws of the Federal Assembly. It is permissible to assume that, in these countries, if the Constitution did not forbid it, the Courts would be entitled to determine whether such laws were in accordance with the Constitution or not.

In some countries although the Constitution is silent upon the question whether the Courts are entitled to interpret it or not, it appears to be the accepted doctrine that Courts should seldom or never embark upon the decision of such questions. Under the Constitution of the Third French Republic the Courts were never called upon to decide whether a legislative or executive act had violated the Constitution, though it may be that it would have been difficult, under that brief and broadly phrased Constitution, to find an opportunity. But it is clear, too, that French jurists thought it improper for a Court to decide whether an act of the legislature conflicted with the Constitution. In their view that was no part of the function of judges. They might decide questions of ordinary law, and in this sphere might, through the *Conseil d'État* as the supreme administrative Court, impose effective checks upon administrative action, but they were not expected to invoke the Constitution. This doctrine appears to prevail under the Fifth Republic, although its Constitution guarantees certain rights and imposes restrictions upon legislative action which were absent from the Constitution of the Third Republic. But, while no ordinary Court is permitted to intervene, the Constitution of the Fifth Republic has established, in Articles 56–63, a Constitutional Council of nine members, three appointed each by the Presidents of the Republic, the Senate, and the National Assembly respectively. Before organic laws may be promulgated or parliamentary standing orders given effect, the Council must examine them to ensure that they do not conflict with the Constitution. The Presidents of the Republic and of the two houses and the Prime Minister may also submit ordinary laws to the Council before they are promulgated. If a provision is declared unconstitutional, it cannot be promulgated or come into force. Although these arrangements go further than those which, in the Constitution of the Fourth Republic (Arts. 91–93), provided for a Constitutional Committee, they fall short of the provision for judicial review as it is found in, say, the United States.

The French doctrine of the function of the judges is accepted in a number of Continental countries. In Holland and Belgium, in Sweden and Denmark, although the Constitutions guarantee rights and by implication forbid the enactment of certain laws, the Courts do not attempt to enforce the Constitution. In the Constitution of the Netherlands, for example, it is declared (Art. 124) that bills passed by the two chambers and assented to by the Sovereign are law. No Court would seek further evidence of their validity. In Norway alone has some attempt been made to review legislation in the Courts, and examples have occurred where laws have been declared void on the ground that they conflicted with some provision of the Constitution. In Sweden the nearest approach there is to judicial review lies in the existence of a body called the Lagrad, composed of three judges of the Supreme Court and one judge of the Supreme Administrative Court, whose duty it is to advise the Riksdag upon important legislation. If the Lagrad advised that a proposed bill were contrary to the Constitution, the Riksdag would almost invariably decline to proceed with it.

It must not be supposed that countries in which the power of judicial review of legislation or of executive action is not practised are indifferent to the supremacy of their Constitutions. In some cases the Constitutions themselves impose no limitations upon the powers of the legislature or executive, and the question of judicial review will not arise. In countries where limitations are imposed, however, it is often held that the only thing to do is to trust the bodies upon which restrictions are imposed to observe these restrictions. Why should judges be thought more trustworthy than legislators or administrators? Or why should judges be thought better equipped to decide what the Constitution means than the members of other institutions of government? And is it not for the people, the source of sovereign power, to determine these questions by their influence upon the legislature and executive? In Switzerland, for example, it is clearly the view of the people and of those who operate the government that the Constitution must be maintained. By the device of the referendum, upon the demand of 30,000 Swiss citizens, a law passed by the National Assembly can be submitted to the people for their approval. Thus, if there is a feeling that some law conflicts with the Constitution, it can be referred to the people, and if approved by them, it has sovereign authority. If it did in fact conflict with the Constitution, its acceptance by the people in a referendum constitutes in effect an amendment of the Constitution.

Although the conscientiousness of legislatures and the vigilance of the people in countries like Switzerland, Holland, Belgium, Norway, Sweden, and Denmark must not be underestimated, it is clear that infractions of the Constitution may pass unheeded or uncorrected. In Switzerland particularly where the federal division of powers adds to the list of limitations upon the legislature found in unitary Constitutions, it is evident that the system of proceeding by referendum is a hit and miss affair. It is not surprising that the idea of judicial review has been discussed increasingly in the countries of Europe, but it is still far from receiving general acceptance.

It is time now to consider how the process of judicial interpretation has worked in those countries where it is accepted. It will be apparent that for the purposes of this discussion the main Constitutions which will fall to be considered are those of the United States, Canada, Australia, and of the constituent provinces or states of those federations, and of Eire. Although there is provision for judicial review in the Constitutions of Latin America, the practice of government there provides little material—save for a few exceptions—upon which to base any description of the process of constitutional change.

It is well to ask first just what is meant by saying that judicial interpretation and decision can change a Constitution. Courts, it must be emphasized, cannot amend a Constitution. They cannot change the words. They must accept the words, and so far as they introduce change, it can come only through their interpretation of the meaning of the words. Courts may, by a series of decisions, elaborate the content of a word or phrase; they may modify or supplement or refine upon their previous decisions; they may even revoke or contradict previous decisions. But throughout they are confined to the words of the Constitution. It is true that, as was remarked in an earlier chapter, these words may sometimes be vague or ambiguous, leaving room for judges to supply from their own minds what the framers of the Constitution might or might not have said; it is true that judges may be fallible, illogical, and changeable in their opinions; it is true that refined distinctions and technical niceties may appear to do violence to common usage and common sense; and it is true, finally, that judges may exceed their proper functions. For all these things judges may be criticized and the system of judicial interpretation itself decried. But the fundamental point to remember is that the judge's proper function is to interpret, not to amend, the words of a statute or of a Constitution, and such changes as Courts may legitimately bring about in the meaning of a Constitution, spring from this function of interpretation, not from any inherent or secret function of law-making.

The nature and importance of judicial interpretation may be judged best, perhaps, if we look at its operation in some concrete cases. The evidence can be obtained, of course, only from those countries where the Constitution is effectively and continuously under judicial review, and this means that, inevitably, the experience

drawn upon is chiefly that of the United States and the members of
the British Commonwealth. Yet, between them, they account for
about one third of the world's population and are not therefore
lightly to be disregarded. Their experience may best be expounded,
perhaps, in terms of certain themes which have been characteristic
of modern developments in Constitutions.

First of all, what part has judicial interpretation played in the
growth of centralization in modern Constitutions? It has been
explained already how changes in economic and technological conditions have led to the increase of the power of central governments
without necessarily causing a change in the actual words of a Constitution. It is interesting to find that these changes in conditions
often obtain recognition in the decisions of judges who find themselves called upon to decide whether an old formula in a Constitution can be made to embrace new and unforeseen circumstances.
They are asked to adapt an old Constitution to new conditions.

One of the best ways of observing this process at work is to trace
the steps by which the Supreme Court of the United States has
interpreted the power given to Congress by the American Constitution to regulate inter-State commerce. When this clause was
introduced into the American Constitution it was thought of essentially as a means by which State tariff barriers could be prevented and
local obstacles against free trade be eliminated. But from the very
first occasion upon which the Supreme Court had an opportunity
to interpret the words of the Constitution regarding inter-State commerce—in the case of *Gibbons* v. *Ogden* (9 Wheaton 1) in 1824—an
ever-widening meaning has been attached to the words. The Constitution said that 'Congress shall have power . . . to regulate commerce . . . among the several States'. In the case of *Gibbons* v. *Ogden*
an attempt was made to persuade the Supreme Court to adopt what
was called a strict construction. The Court, through the mouth of
Chief Justice Marshall, rejected the proposal. It had been asked to
say that commerce was limited 'to traffic, to buying, and selling, or
the interchange of commodities' and could not include navigation.
'Commerce,' the Court said (at pp. 189-90), 'undoubtedly, is traffic,
but it is something more: it is intercourse. It describes the commercial intercourse between nations, and parts of nations, in all its
branches, and is regulated by prescribing rules for carrying on that

intercourse.' Next it had to be decided what commerce 'among the
several States' meant. The Court was clear that this must include
some power of regulating commerce inside a State. 'Commerce
among the States cannot stop at the external boundary-line of each
State, but may be introduced into the interior.' There were some
limits, however. 'It is not intended to say,' the Court declared (at
pp. 194–5), 'that these words comprehend that commerce which is
completely internal, which is carried on between man and man in
a State, or between different parts of the same State, and which does
not extend to or affect other States. Such a power would be incon-
venient, and is certainly unnecessary. Comprehensive as the word
"among" is, it may very properly be restricted to that commerce
which concerns more States than one. . . . The completely internal
commerce of a State, then, may be considered as reserved for the
State itself.' And finally, what did 'regulate' mean? 'This power,'
said the Court (at p. 196), 'like all others vested in Congress, is
complete in itself, may be exercised to its utmost extent, and
acknowledges no limitations other than are prescribed in the
Constitution.'

In the decades that followed the Court was asked to decide on
many occasions just where inter-State commerce ended and intra-
State commerce began. The industrial, commercial, and transport
revolutions, which converted the United States into one closely
interlocked economic and social system, made it extremely difficult
to answer this question. The Court adopted successive formulae,
but all had the common characteristic of extending the power of
Congress. In 1914, in The Shreveport case (Houston, E. & W. Texas
Railway Co. v. United States (234 U.S. 342)), the Court said (at pp.
351–2) that 'wherever the inter-state and intra-state transactions . . .
are so related that the government of the one involves the control
of the other, it is Congress, and not the State, that is entitled to
prescribe the final and dominant rule. . . .' In 1922 in the case of
Stafford v. Wallace (258 U.S. 495), the Court declared (at pp. 518–19)
that there were 'streams of commerce from one part of the country
to another, which are ever flowing', and that it would not attempt
to prevent Congress from controlling them 'by a nice and technical
inquiry into the non-inter-state character of some of its necessary
incidents and facilities when considered alone and without reference

to their association with the movement of which they were an essential but subordinate part'.

By 1937, when the Court decided the case of the *National Labour Relations Board* v. *Jones and Laughlin Steel Corporation* (301 U.S. 1), the idea of a 'stream' or 'flow' of commerce was becoming outmoded. 'The congressional authority to protect inter-state commerce from burdens and obstructions is not limited to transactions which can be deemed to be an essential part of a "flow" of inter-state or foreign commerce. . . . Although activities may be intra-state in character when separately considered, if they have such a close and substantial relation to inter-state commerce that their control is essential or appropriate to protect that commerce from burdens and obstructions, Congress cannot be denied the power to exercise that control' (at pp. 36 and 37).

In some cases, of which *The Schechter Poultry Corporation* case (295 U.S. 495) in 1935 is one example, the Court had spoken (at pp. 546-8) of the distinction between intra-State transactions which 'directly' affected inter-State commerce and those which affected it only 'indirectly' and appeared to regard the former as falling under the commerce power. But in two decisions, in 1941 and 1942, these refinements were left behind. In the case of *United States* v. *Darby* (312 U.S. 100) in 1941 the Court said (at p. 118): 'The power of Congress over inter-state commerce is not confined to the regulation of commerce among the states. It extends to those activities intra-state which so affect inter-state commerce or the exercise of the power of Congress over it as to make regulation of them appropriate means to the attainment of a legitimate end, the exercise of the granted power of Congress to regulate inter-state commerce.' And finally in the case of *Wichard* v. *Filburn* (317 U.S. 111) in 1942 the Court said (at p. 125): 'Even if [an] activity be local and though it may not be regarded as commerce, it may still, whatever its nature, be reached by Congress if it exerts a substantial economic effect on inter-state commerce, and this irrespective of whether such effect is what might at some earlier time have been defined as "direct" or "indirect".'

As we follow the decisions of the Supreme Court on this matter, it does not seem to be an exaggeration to say that it has adapted the commerce power of Congress to all the demands of the economic, commercial, industrial, and transport revolutions of the past one hundred and fifty years. Congress indeed has powers far wider than it wishes to exercise. Not that the Court has always upheld Congressional statutes in the field of commerce. In 1935, in *The Schechter Poultry Corporation case*, the Court unanimously rejected an important part of the New Deal legislation sponsored by President Franklin D. Roosevelt, on the ground that it attempted to regulate activities which did not fall within the commerce power. To the argument that these activities were inextricably interwoven with inter-State commerce, two judges—Mr Justice Cardozo and Mr Justice Stone—answered (295 U.S. 495 at p. 554): 'To find immediacy or directness here is to find it almost everywhere. If centripetal forces are to be isolated to the exclusion of the forces that oppose and counteract them, there will be an end to our federal system.' The Court continually asserts that there are some limits on the commerce power; it admits that it is difficult in many cases to draw the line; but it accepts the duty to do so. It said in 1937, in *The Jones and Laughlin Steel Corporation case*: 'Undoubtedly the scope of this power must be considered in the light of our dual system of government and may not be extended so as to embrace effects upon inter-state commerce so indirect and remote that to embrace them, in view of our complex society, would effectually obliterate the distinction between what is national and what is local and create a completely centralized government' (301 U.S. 1 at p. 37).

Yet, in spite of occasional setbacks from the Supreme Court, Congress lacks no power to control modern economic life. So extensive has the commerce power proved to be that it has been unnecessary in the United States to contemplate an amendment of the Constitution to adjust the powers of Congress in economic affairs to the needs of the United States today. It is indeed remarkable that powers granted over one hundred and fifty years ago to an agricultural country with a few million people should be adapted to the needs of a great industrial power with thirty times that population. That the Constitution has been adapted to the new society is the work of the Supreme Court.

Let it be noticed, however, that the Supreme Court could make this adaptation because the words of the Constitution were adaptable. If we look at the Canadian Constitution, on the other hand,

we find a difference, and a difference which is surprising. For the
Canadian Constitution gives to the parliament of Canada power to
make laws concerning 'the regulation of trade and commerce'. Here
is a wide grant of power, with no restriction like that in the United
States to 'among the several States'. Yet other restrictions have been
found. The Constitution grants to the provinces exclusive power to
make laws concerning 'property and civil rights in a province'. It
seems obvious to a layman that these two phrases could conflict,
and in fact the Courts were obliged to decide how they were to be
interpreted. The outcome of judicial decision was that the words
'trade and commerce' must be construed so as not to conflict with
'property and civil rights', which has meant that the former phrase
has been construed narrowly and the latter widely. It may well be
objected that the Courts could have adopted a different line of
argument; they could have given a pre-eminence to the words
'trade and commerce'. There is some truth in this, but at the same
time the existence of the provision that a province had exclusive
power to make laws on property and civil rights was an obstacle.
The Canadian Constitution was not easily adaptable, even had the
judges been ready to adapt.

What has been said of the interpretation of the trade and commerce power in the Canadian Constitution applies generally to the
whole story of judicial interpretation of the Canadian Constitution.
Whereas in the United States the central legislature has been able to
acquire substantially all the powers it has needed to regulate affairs
of national concern through the process of judicial interpretation,
in Canada the Courts have tended to magnify the powers of the
provinces as against the centre. It must be emphasized that, before
an opinion can be expressed upon the significance of this difference,
account must be taken of the fact that the terms of the Canadian
Constitution differ in important respects from the American. Yet
something must be allowed also for a difference in attitude on the
part of the judges who have chosen, in the United States, to use their
legitimate discretion in favour of the Union, and, in Canada, in
favour of the provinces. It is of interest perhaps to add that up to
1950 the last word in the interpretation of the Canadian Constitution lay with the Judicial Committee of the Privy Council,
sitting in London and composed almost invariably of British judges

with no first-hand experience of legal and political life in Canada. However when every allowance is made for this element of human discretion, it must be asserted that there are legal obstacles in the Canadian Constitution to the extension of the power of the parliament of Canada which even a Canadian Supreme Court, endowed with the last word in interpretation, will find it difficult to remove by the process of judicial interpretation.

There is a further point to be considered in discussing the interpretation of the commerce power by the Supreme Court of the United States. The Court has given its decisions upon a background of economic integration which must influence its opinion. There is, in fact, a very great deal of commerce among the several States in the American Union. It has increased in intensity and extent, particularly in the last fifty years. More and more transactions have come within the sphere of inter-State commerce, and it has become harder and harder to draw the line where the powers of Congress should cease. This fact has, quite legitimately, been reflected in judicial decisions upon the cases that come before the Court. In a country like Australia, however, where similar powers are conferred upon the parliament of the Commonwealth, there has not been so much inter-State commerce to regulate. The High Court has certainly given the widest signification to the term, but the facts of economic life, particularly the concentration of a large part of the population in the capital cities of the States and the carrying on of a great deal of commerce intra-State, have led to a smaller proportion of the country's economic affairs being capable of regulation under the commerce power.

This is not to say that the trend of judicial decision in Australia has been against the growth of central powers. In fact, by the interpretation of certain powers, other than that over inter-State commerce, it has been possible for a wide sphere of industrial life to be placed under the regulation of the Commonwealth and indeed for the whole system of government to become more centralized than that of the United States or Canada. A word should be said about one important decision in the sphere of public finance. In 1942 the High Court of Australia upheld legislation which, in effect, obliged the States to relinquish their powers to impose income tax and to accept in return grants from the Commonwealth parliament.

(*South Australia* v. *the Commonwealth*, 65 C.L.R. 373.) By this decision the seal was set upon a course of action under which, if the Commonwealth wished, most of the political independence of the States could be destroyed.

The effect of judicial decision in assisting the centralization of government may be illustrated in another sphere, and that is in the exercise of the war power or the power to control defence. The general result of judicial interpretation in all three federations—the United States, Australia, and Canada—has been to assert that the central parliament has the fullest powers to wage war and to provide for defence. It is true that, from time to time, a measure has been declared invalid on the ground that it was not warranted under the defence power, and it is true also that inconsistencies can be discovered in the judgements of the Courts in these cases. But it is rare to find a case where action is frustrated by the Courts, at any rate while war is actually raging. In time of peace Courts look more unfavourably upon legislation which in the guise of the defence power attempts to invade the spheres of the States.

It is interesting to observe the way in which judicial decision comes to co-operate with the process of formal amendment in bringing about change in a Constitution. Sometimes a judicial decision will create a situation which leads to a movement to amend the Constitution. The Sixteenth Amendment of the American Constitution came about in this way. The Constitution had laid it down that no direct tax should be levied except in proportion to the population. Now income tax cannot effectively be levied in this way and it was therefore a matter of some moment to Congress to decide whether income tax was a direct tax or not. In 1895 the Supreme Court decided (*Pollock* v. *Farmers' Loan & Trust Co.*, 157 U.S. 429 and 158 U.S. 601) that it was a direct tax and as a result the power to raise it had practically no value. The difficulty was overcome by the passing of the Sixteenth Amendment, in 1913, which removed these restrictions upon the power of Congress to levy income tax. ·

Sometimes a judicial decision allies itself with a constitutional amendment to change a Constitution. Thus in Australia the predominant position of the Commonwealth parliament in the financial affairs of the country has been achieved by the combined effect of a formal amendment of the Constitution which was carried in 1928 and which increased the power of the Commonwealth in financial affairs and also of the judicial decision of 1942 concerning income tax which has recently been referred to. What is interesting in the United States is that the actual increase of central power by formal amendment is slight whereas the effect of judicial decision is great. In Australia, though amendments have been few, they have been of sufficient importance to justify being accorded almost an equal share with judicial interpretation in the growth of centralization.

A predominant trend in the development of modern Constitutions, next only in importance to the growth of centralization, is the growth in the relative power of the executive branch. How far has this trend been assisted or checked by the interpretation which the judicial branch has placed upon those parts of a Constitution which lay down the powers of the executive? In the Constitution of the United States it is declared that 'all legislative powers herein granted shall be vested in a Congress of the United States'. Now in most modern states it has been found necessary to empower the executive, especially in times of war or other emergency, to make rules which appear to have all or most of the characteristics of legislation. The parliament delegates legislative power to a minister or a department or an official. Can this be done in the United States? Does not the Constitution, by implication at any rate, forbid the delegation by Congress of its legislative power to any other body? This question has been raised in the Courts on a number of occasions when the validity of the exercise of rule-making power by the President or some administrative agency has been called in question. The answer of the Supreme Court has been that, while Congress cannot delegate its legislative power to another agency, it may authorize other agencies to exercise rule-making powers of a very wide range and variety, provided they fall short of being legislative in nature. This means that the Court has had to say what 'legislative' means, and to determine, in particular cases, whether a delegated power amounts to a power to legislate. Broadly speaking, the Supreme Court has ruled that Congress, when authorizing another agency to exercise rule-making power, must embody in the authorizing act the principles or standards which are to be followed or applied.

The interpretation which the Supreme Court has adopted is best summed up in the following passage from the judgement of

Chief Justice Stone, delivered in 1944 in the case of *Yakus* v. *United States* (321 U.S. 414). He said (at pp. 424-5, 426):

The Constitution as a continuously operative charter of government does not demand the impossible or the impracticable. It does not require that Congress find for itself every fact upon which it desires to base legislative action or that it make for itself detailed determinations which it has declared to be prerequisite to the application of the legislative policy to particular facts and circumstances impossible for Congress itself properly to investigate. The essentials of the legislative function are the determination of the legislative policy and its formulation and promulgation as a defined and binding rule of conduct. . . . These essentials are preserved when Congress has specified the basic conditions of fact upon whose existence or occurrence, ascertained from relevant data by a designated administrative agency, it directs that its statutory command shall be effective. It is no objection that the determination of facts and the inferences to be drawn from them in the light of the statutory standards and declaration of policy call for the exercise of judgment, and for the formulation of subsidiary administrative policy within the prescribed statutory framework. . . . Only if we could say that there is an absence of standards for the guidance of the administrator's action, so that it would be impossible in a proper proceeding to ascertain whether the will of Congress has been obeyed, would we be justified in overriding its choice of means for effecting its declared purpose. . . .

The number of occasions upon which the Supreme Court has felt obliged to declare that an Act of Congress was invalid on these grounds has been very few. None had occurred until 1935, when in two cases in that year (*Panama Refining Co.* v. *Ryan*, 293 U.S. 388, and *Schechter Poultry Corp.* v. *United States*, 295 U.S. 495) parts of the National Industrial Recovery Act, upon which President Franklin Roosevelt's New Deal was based, were declared invalid, on the ground that they delegated legislative power to other agencies. They delegated a rule-making power which, in the words of Mr Justice Cardozo in the second of the two cases (he had dissented in the first case), was 'unconfined and vagrant' and was 'not canalized within banks to keep it from overflowing' (at p. 551). But since 1935 no further act has been held invalid on these grounds —a remarkable situation when it is remembered that throughout the years 1941-5 the United States was at war and a vast rule-making power was exercised by the President and by administrative agencies under the authority of Acts of Congress. The Supreme Court upheld them all when cases came before it.

It is clear that the attitude of the Supreme Court has made possible in the United States a flexibility in the exercise of rule-making power which a strict view of the nature of legislative power and of the words of the Constitution would have prevented. The Court has deliberately adopted the view that these portions of the Constitution must be construed flexibly. And it has been ready to admit, in the words of Mr Justice Stone in 1941, that 'in an increasingly complex society Congress obviously could not perform its functions if it were obliged to find all the facts subsidiary to the basic conclusions which support the defined legislative policy. . . .' (*Opp Cotton Mills* v. *Administrator*, 312 U.S. 126 at p. 145.)

If the Supreme Court of the United States has been prepared to sanction a wide use of rule-making power by the executive, in the face of the terms of the Constitution of the United States, it is not surprising to discover that in Australia and Canada the Courts have refused to accept the contention that parliament cannot delegate legislative power. The tradition of the separation of powers has little or no force in these two federations with their parliamentary executives. The same is true of other members of the British Commonwealth, like South Africa and New Zealand. Although the Constitutions in all these countries place legislative power in the hands of the King, or his representative, and the parliament, and although an attempt has been made from time to time to argue before the Courts that this legislative power cannot be delegated, the Courts have refused to adopt such a position. In many cases they seem to have been influenced towards this decision by the existence of the parliamentary executive. (See Evatt J. in a case in 1931 before the Australian High Court, *Victorian Stevedoring Co.* v. *Dignan*, 46 C.L.R. 73 at p. 114.) Occasionally a logically minded judge admits that the terms of the Constitution might support an argument against delegation. Mr Justice Dixon stated this view in his judgement in the case just mentioned, when he said (at pp. 101-2): 'It may be acknowledged that the manner in which the Constitution accomplished the separation of powers does logically or theoretically make the Parliament the exclusive repository of the legislative power of the Commonwealth. The existence in Parliament of power to authorize subordinate legislation may be ascribed to a conception of that legislative power which depends less upon juristic analysis and perhaps more upon the history and usages of British legislation and the theories of English law.' This whole judgement is a most illuminating exposition of the difference between the Constitution of the United States and the Constitutions within the British Commonwealth. As a rule, however, judges have not felt it necessary to argue the point at length. They have adopted the position which the first Chief Justice of the Australian High Court took up when he said in 1909 that 'it is too late in the day to contend that such a delegation, if it is a delegation, is objectionable in any sense'. (Griffith C.J. in *Baxter* v. *Ah Way*, 8 C.L.R. 626 at pp. 632–3.)

It is worth while to consider, if only briefly, the way in which, by judicial interpretation, the provisions of a Constitution guaranteeing the rights of the individual or of communities or associations, are developed. This is a large subject and it will be possible to illustrate only one or two aspects of it. The experience of Ireland under the Constitution of 1937, is interesting because it illustrates very well the extent to which Courts have an opportunity to interpret or safeguard the rights of the individual. In a series of cases which came before the Supreme Court of Eire in the years from 1940 to 1950 attempts were made to assert that the Constitution guaranteed certain rights and that the legislature or the executive had acted unconstitutionally in transgressing those rights.

Four cases came before the Irish Supreme Court in the period from 1940 to 1942. (*In the matter of offences against the State (Amendment) Bill, 1940*, [1940] I.R. 470; In re *McGrath & Harte*, [1941] I.R. 68; In re *Thomas MacCurtain*, [1941] I.R. 83; *State (Walsh and others)* v. *Lennon*, [1942] I.R. 112.) In each of these cases the Court was asked to say that the legislature or the executive had acted in denial of the rights of the subject either because it authorized or because it carried out the detention of persons without trial, or their trial without a jury or by military tribunals or undertook the forcible entry of houses or seizure of documents. In each case the Court was obliged to say that the words of the Constitution fully justified these actions. Rights were no doubt declared in the Constitution, but at the same time they were qualified by other sections of the Constitution. The words of the Constitution were so plain and sweeping that the Court could not hold otherwise.

In contrast to these cases, may be considered two others in which certain precise provisions of the Constitution came under discussion and in which the Court was entitled to express an opinion. In 1943 the Court was asked to consider the School Attendance Bill, 1942, which empowered the Minister of Education to lay down and require certain standards of education in respect of children not attending school. The Court decided that, in so far as this Bill empowered the Minister to require more than a minimum standard of education and to certify the manner in which such education should be received, it was invalid, for it conflicted with Article 42 (3) of the Constitution. That Article said: 'The State shall, however, as guardian of the common good, require in view of actual conditions that the children receive a certain minimum education, moral, intellectual and social.' In the Court's view this provision must be construed strictly. The State could require that children shall receive a minimum of education; so long as parents supply this minimum, the manner in which it is given is not a matter in which, under the Constitution, the State is entitled to interfere. (Re *School Attendance Bill, 1942*, [1943] I.R. 334.)

In 1947 the Irish Supreme Court was asked to consider the meaning of the provision in the Constitution (Article 40 (6)) which guaranteed the right of the citizens to form associations and unions. The declaration of this right is followed by the proviso: 'Laws, however, may be enacted for the regulation and control in the public interest of the exercise of the foregoing right.' This looks rather like an 'escape clause' of the kind so familiar in the Irish Constitution and in many others. The Irish parliament passed an Act which restricted the right of citizens to form unions and the Supreme Court had to decide whether it was valid or not. (*National Union of Railwaymen* v. *Irish Transport and General Workers' Union*, [1947] I.R. 77.) On the one hand it could be contended that the Act was contrary to the guaranteed right to form associations; on the other that it was justifiable as a law to regulate or control the exercise of the right in the public interest. The Supreme Court, reversing the decision of the High Court from which the case had come on appeal, held that the Act was invalid on the ground that, far from being an act to control the exercise of the right to form associations, it attempted to abolish that right altogether. Here was a case where there was room for a difference of opinion, and it showed itself in the difference of view between the High Court and the Supreme Court.

A great part of the history of the Supreme Court of the United States is concerned with the interpretation and enforcement of individual rights in the Constitution—a task of great difficulty as the discussion in Chapter 3 has already indicated. It must suffice for our purpose here to illustrate the way in which, by judicial interpretation, certain phrases in the Constitution have come to be given a precise and detailed significance. The best example, perhaps, is the Supreme Court's interpretation of the provisions in the Fifth and Fourteenth Amendments to the Constitution that no person be 'deprived of life, liberty, or property, without due process of law'. At first glance it might be expected that the phrase 'due process of law' means no more than 'in accordance with the law' or 'save as provided by law'—expressions which occur in many modern Constitutions and contain no necessary guarantee of good government. No doubt it was open to the Supreme Court of the United States to adopt this view and to regard the provisions of any law duly passed by Congress or a State legislature as a justification for any action taken to deprive a citizen of life, liberty, or property, provided of course it did not conflict with any prohibition in the Constitution. In fact the Supreme Court has refused to stand aside in this way. It has regarded 'due process of law' as a phrase which guarantees the recognition of certain rights, and it has been prepared to say, in particular cases, what these rights are and whether they have been denied or recognized.

Thus the Court has held that the due process of law involves the right, at least in a capital case, of an accused person to be defended by counsel and that the denial of this right invalidates a trial (*Powell* v. *Alabama*, 287 U.S. 45 (1932)); that a conviction based upon confessions extorted from the accused under duress was a denial of due process (*Chambers* v. *Florida*, 309 U.S. 227 (1940), *Ashcraft* v. *Tennessee*, 322 U.S. 143 (1944)); and that a conviction obtained from a jury which was obviously overawed by mob violence was in conflict with due process and could not stand (*Moore* v. *Dempsey*,

261 U.S. 86 (1923)). Expressed in general terms, the Supreme Court has regarded the due process clause as requiring that governmental action 'shall be consistent with the fundamental principles of liberty and justice which lie at the base of all our civil and political institutions and not infrequently are designated as "the law of the land" '. (*Hebert* v. *Louisiana*, 272 U.S. 312 at p. 316 (1926).) 'As applied to a criminal trial, denial of due process is the failure to observe that fundamental fairness essential to the very concept of justice.' (*Lisenba* v. *California*, 314 U.S. 219 at p. 236 (1941).)

When the task before the Supreme Court is considered, and the history of its work is reviewed, it is not difficult to endorse the words which Alexis de Tocqueville used in his *Democracy in America* in 1835: 'The Federal judges must not only be good citizens, and men possessed of that information and integrity which are indispensable to magistrates, but they must be statesmen—politicians, not unread in the signs of the times, not afraid to brave the obstacles which can be subdued, nor slow to turn aside such encroaching elements as may threaten the supremacy of the Union and the obedience which is due to the laws.' And he added, 'if the Supreme Court is ever composed of imprudent men or bad citizens, the Union may be plunged into anarchy or civil war'. What he said of the Supreme Court of the United States, applies with almost equal force to other countries where judicial review of the Constitution prevails.

When the effect of judicial decision upon Constitutions is studied, it is natural to ask: Should this function be placed upon the Courts? It is possible to understand why judges are obliged to take these decisions—it arises inevitably as part of their duty to say what the law is in a case of dispute. But it brings them into the field of political controversy and it means, too, that their appointments are criticized and canvassed and that those who appoint them are inclined to consider what views they are likely to take of the interpretation of the Constitution. Does this not discredit the judiciary? There can be little doubt that there is some truth in this opinion, though it is interesting to notice that in the United States, Canada, and Australia, the supreme tribunals are regarded with respect, though often with sympathy for their difficulties in the task laid upon them.

What is the alternative? One line is to say that the Courts must accept the laws of the legislature as valid and that those who do not like them may unite to have them referred to the people in a referendum. This in fact is the Swiss position, so far as federal laws are concerned. It works with fair success in Switzerland. But could it be worked, say, for the whole of the American Union? And is it not also, in effect, an alternative method of amending a Constitution? It is argued sometimes, too, that it is best to rely upon public opinion to control the legislature and to leave the electors at the polls to punish its members if they exceed their powers. There is not much consolation here to a minority which hopes to see its rights protected by a Constitution. Suggestions that these decisions should be taken not by judges in the ordinary Courts but by some specially constituted tribunal, of which the Constitutional Council of the Fifth French Republic is an example, have the advantage that they remove political controversies from the Courts where questions of ordinary law alone may be decided, but they leave untouched the difficulty that in fact this tribunal must pronounce upon the ordinary law because it is required to say whether or not it conflicts with the Constitution.

It seems certain that if the requirements of a Constitution are to be regularly enforced, resort to the Courts and subsequent judicial decision are usually unavoidable. The Swiss appear to have the best alternative, but it should be appreciated that it is difficult to work and that the Swiss have an experience and a skill in this form of government which may not transplant easily to foreign soil. Moreover it is to be emphasized that even in Switzerland all the actions of cantonal authorities, which incidentally possess powers in criminal law, are subject to the control of the Courts. What is clear, however, is that if Courts are to undertake this work, they cannot be expected to work effectively if they are charged with the interpretation of a Constitution which is expressed in vague and emotional phrases. The success of judicial review depends as much upon a well-drafted Constitution as upon the calibre of the judges themselves.

8

How Constitutions Change: Usage and Convention

THE PROCESSES OF constitutional change which have been discussed in the two preceding chapters have this in common, that the changes they produce in the law of a Constitution are recognized and applied by the Courts. They are changes of the law in the eyes of the law. In this chapter we consider a process of change which certainly affects the law of the Constitution, sometimes by making it in practice a dead letter, sometimes by determining the way in which in practice it will be interpreted or exercised, but which, none the less, leaves its words unchanged and its meaning or interpretation unchanged so far as the Courts are concerned. By usage and convention the law of a Constitution, strictly so called, is supplemented by a whole collection of rules which, though not part of the law, are accepted as binding, and which regulate political institutions in a country and clearly form a part of the system of government.

It is important that some study should be made of these non-legal rules in their relation to a Constitution because it is often thought that they operate solely or, at any rate mainly, in countries which have no Constitution. This view has arisen no doubt from the stress which is laid upon the influence and importance of constitutional usage and convention in the working of government in England, a stress which has led people to speak as if the principal rules which govern the government in England are non-legal rules. In fact this is not a true picture of the relative importance of legal and non-legal rules in England—the Representation of the People Acts from 1832

E

to 1948 are surely as important as the conventions which regulate cabinet government. Quite apart from the position in England, however, it is essential to realize that in all countries usage and convention are important and that in many countries which have Constitutions usage and convention play as important a part as they do in England. It is interesting to notice that A. V. Dicey, whose *Law of the Constitution*, first published in 1885, gave the classic exposition of the significance of constitutional conventions in England, was well aware of this. 'It may be asserted without much exaggeration,' he wrote, 'that the conventional element in the Constitution of the United States is as large as in the English Constitution.'

A word must be said about the distinction that is intended by the employment of the two words 'usage' and 'convention'. By 'convention' is meant a binding rule, a rule of behaviour accepted as obligatory by those concerned in the working of the Constitution; by usage is meant no more than a usual practice. Clearly a usage might become a convention. What is usually done comes to be what is done. It is often difficult to say whether a particular course of conduct is obligatory or persuasive only, and it is convenient in such a case to be able to say that it is certainly a usage and probably or doubtfully, as the case may be, a convention.

Conventions appear to arise from at least two sources. Sometimes, as just indicated, a course of conduct may be persisted in over a long period of time and gradually attain first persuasive and then obligatory force. It is common to call conventions of this kind 'customs'. But a convention may arise much more quickly than this. There may be an agreement among the people concerned to work in a particular way and to adopt a particular rule of conduct. This rule is immediately binding and it is a convention. It has not arisen from custom; it has had no previous history as a usage. It springs from agreement. Its basis is indeed very like that of the conventions which are drawn up in international relations. They are held to be morally binding and politically binding, but until they are enacted by the appropriate machinery of a state they do not in most countries alter the law or form part of the law.

A discussion of conventions which arise from agreement reminds us of the fact that such conventions might easily be written down. They might take the form of an agreement signed by the leaders of political parties, or of a memorandum issued after discussions between ministers. Conventions are not necessarily unwritten rules, though those which have grown up by custom often are. It is important to stress this fact for it illustrates once again how unsatisfactory are distinctions among constitutional rules between 'written' and 'unwritten'. It is a distinction which is seldom applied accurately and is seldom, if ever, profitable.

A large and important part of the conventional rules in some systems of government is found in the standing orders of the two houses of the legislature and these, of course, are all written down. In some countries, it must be admitted, these rules are enacted and form part of the law in the ordinary sense; in a few, of which Finland and Sweden are examples, they are to be found in a supreme organic law which is in fact, if not in form, a part of the Constitution. But in many countries they are the result of resolutions passed by each house in the exercise of its right to regulate its own proceedings, and as such are not part of the law strictly so called. It must be admitted that some authorities have argued that the standing orders of the houses of legislature are not conventions but are part of the law, even when they are passed only by resolutions of the houses concerned. They are thought in some cases to form part of a special branch of the law which governs the proceedings of the legislature. It may be that this argument can be sustained in some cases, but there are others where the standing orders are not part of the law and where it seems legitimate to regard them as conventions, and written conventions at that.

The distinctions which have been drawn in the preceding paragraphs will be illustrated when we come to consider the various ways in which usage and convention operate to affect the law of the Constitution. The first way in which usage and convention show their effects is in nullifying a provision of a Constitution. This might be expressed by saying that convention paralyses the arm of the law. It is essential to stress that it does not amend or abolish the law. It does not amputate the limb; it merely makes its use impossible. A well-known example of this effect of convention is found in the fact that in many Constitutions the legal power of the head of the State to veto or refuse his assent to laws passed by the legislature is nullified by convention. In the Constitutions of Denmark, Norway, and

Sweden, the King is given certain powers to refuse assent to bills passed by the legislature, but in all three cases it is now agreed that he may not exercise these powers. The last occasion upon which the King of Denmark refused assent to a bill was in 1865, and although the King of Sweden vetoed a bill in 1912, he acted on that occasion upon the advice of his ministers. In Holland and Belgium similarly the power of the monarch to veto legislation has been nullified by convention.

In the Constitutions of those members of the British Commonwealth which have retained the monarchical form of government, it is usual to find powers granted either to the Queen or to her representative, the Governor-General, to refuse his assent to a bill. In all these cases it is accepted that, by convention, this power will not be exercised. In certain Constitutions in the Commonwealth, too, provisions are found which empower a Governor-General to reserve a bill for the signification of the Queen's pleasure, or, yet again, which empower the Queen to disallow an act which has been duly passed by the parliament of a member of the Commonwealth and assented to by the Governor-General. Powers of this kind are found in the Constitutions of Canada, Australia, and New Zealand, for example. By convention, however, it is agreed that the Queen would take no action in regard to a reserved bill contrary to the wishes of the government of the member of the Commonwealth concerned, and that her exercise of the power of disallowance is no longer possible.

It is interesting, perhaps, to remark that the convention by which the Governor-General's power to veto a bill is nullified is based really upon custom—custom which was developed in Britain and has long been transported across the seas—and is not inscribed in any written document. The conventions concerning the powers of reservation and disallowance, however, though a product of custom in a large measure, were committed to writing by the Imperial Conference of 1930. They constitute in large measure a recognition of an existing custom, but in addition they represent an agreement between governments and an undertaking by the government of the United Kingdom in particular that it would not advise the Queen to exercise her legal powers of veto and disallowance contrary to the wishes of the Dominions. Doubtless it was in large part because an agreement between governments was involved, that the convention was recognized and confirmed in writing.

An interesting example of the way in which a legal power can be nullified by convention was provided by the working of the Constitution of the Third French Republic. It contained a provision that the President of the Republic might, with the consent of the Senate, dissolve the Chamber of Deputies. This power was exercised once, in 1877, two years after the inauguration of the Republic, by President MacMahon, and it was never exercised again, nor was it thought proper that it should be exercised again. The circumstances in which MacMahon dissolved the Chamber and the controversy that followed it made it appear that any attempt by the President to dissolve would constitute an attack upon the Republican régime. By custom too the President soon came to occupy a place in the Constitution comparable to that of a monarch in a democratic kingdom, and his power to initiate action of this kind had become nullified.

The Third French Republic and the United States provided an interesting example of what appeared to be a nullification of legal powers conferred, or at any rate not denied, in the Constitution, about which it is possible to have some argument. These were the alleged limitations imposed by convention upon re-election to the office of President. In the Constitution of the Third Republic it was stated that the President of the Republic would be elected by an absolute majority in a joint meeting of the Senate and the Chamber of Deputies, and that he would be eligible for re-election. In the American Constitution no restriction appeared upon the right of a President to stand for re-election. What happened in practice? Up to 1939 it appeared to have become an established convention in France that the President should not stand for re-election, but should content himself with one term of office (seven years) and, in the United States, that a President should not stand for re-election more than once. In 1939, however, the President of the French Republic, M. Lebrun, was re-elected to a second term of office at the expiry of his first term of seven years and in 1940 Franklin D. Roosevelt was elected for a third term as President of the United States and, in 1944, for a fourth. What is the significance of these events? Does it mean that what appeared in France up to 1939 and in the United

States up to 1940 to be a convention was in fact only a usage? Or is it more accurate to say that the convention existed up to that date and was amended or abolished or even broken by the action taken in 1939 in France and in 1940 in the United States? Or is the true explanation that the convention merely laid down that, as a general rule and in normal times, re-election for a second term in France and for a third term in the United States should not occur, it being understood that exceptional circumstances permitted and justified exceptions to the general rule? This last explanation gains support from the fact that in France in 1939 those who proposed the re-election of M. Lebrun justified it on the ground of the critical state of European affairs, while in the United States in 1940 President Roosevelt's standing for re-election for a third term was justified by the need for continuity in the direction of the affairs of the United States when the danger of war was imminent, an argument which in 1944 was still stronger for the United States by then was fully involved in the war.

It seems proper to conclude that in both France and the United States, therefore, a convention against re-election for a second and a third term respectively was established. French Presidents usually recognized this by announcing upon election that they would not stand for re-election. In the United States there was always some doubt whether a Vice-President who succeeded to the office upon the death of a President, and could claim therefore that he had not been elected as President and had in any case not had a full term as President, might stand for election for two terms in his own right. But apart from this ambiguity, there is little doubt that there was a convention against a third term. The re-election of President Roosevelt for a third and then a fourth term has indeed confirmed the belief among politicians in the United States that the rule embodied in this convention was good and steps have been taken, as will be explained later, to turn this convention into law. In the Fifth French Republic, it is to be observed that the Constitution is silent upon the question of the re-election of a President. It will be interesting to see whether any usage or convention grows up to limit a President to a single term and nullify his right to stand for re-election.

Though convention sometimes nullifies the law of the Constitution, and renders it impossible for powers granted therein to be exercised at all, it does not always go so far as this. What often happens is that powers granted in a Constitution are indeed exercised but that, while they are in law exercised by those to whom they are granted, they are in practice exercised by some other person or body of persons. Convention, in short, transfers powers granted in a Constitution from one person to another.

A first illustration of this transfer of power is found in the way in which, in countries which have a system of cabinet government, ministers are appointed. In many of these countries the King has the power in law to appoint ministers; in practice, by convention, he appoints those persons whom the Prime Minister recommends to him. There is no doubt that the King exercises the legal power conferred upon him in the Constitution; there is no question of nullification of legal power; but its exercise is governed by the advice of the Prime Minister. A glance at the Constitution of Canada illustrates the point. The Constitution—the British North America Act, 1867 —says that 'there shall be a Council to aid and advise in the government of Canada, to be styled the Queen's Privy Council for Canada; and the persons who are to be members of that Council shall be from time to time chosen and summoned by the Governor-General and sworn in as Privy Councillors, and members thereof may be from time to time removed by the Governor-General'. There is the law and it gives a clear and unfettered power to the Queen's representative, the Governor-General, to appoint whom he pleases to aid and advise him in the government of Canada. In practice, by convention, the Governor-General appoints ministers on the advice of the Prime Minister. What is true in Canada, is true also—with minor modifications and variations in the degree to which law and convention regulate the matter—in Australia, New Zealand, and South Africa, for example, and in the Scandinavian monarchies and in Holland and Belgium.

In most countries where cabinet government or the system of the parliamentary executive is in operation it is found that convention operates to transfer the legal powers of the head of the state to other hands in the practical working of government. In the appointment of the Prime Minister himself, in the exercise of the power to dissolve the legislature, in the exercise of executive powers, and notably in the exercise of the powers to declare war, to conduct foreign relations or to make appointments, it is common to find that such powers as the head of the state possesses by the law of the Constitution are exercised, by convention, upon the advice and initiative of others, and for this exercise these others are responsible. It is not practicable to generalize upon the extent to which convention regulates this transfer in each country. Constitutions differ in the extent to which they prescribe certain procedures in the exercise of these powers. Moreover it is difficult, where usage and convention admittedly operate, to state precisely how far usage and how far convention exists, or to formulate the usage and convention in words. What can be asserted with confidence, however, is that usage and convention do operate, in varying degree in different countries, to bring about this transfer of the practical exercise of legal power to other hands.

It may be worth while to illustrate the difficulty of formulating conventions in these matters by giving an example. Take the case of the exercise by the representative of the Queen in a member of the British Commonwealth of the undoubted legal power conferred upon him by the Constitution to dissolve parliament. It would probably be agreed without much argument that this power must be exercised only on the advice of a Prime Minister, though even then there is some room for disagreement about whether a Prime Minister may act either without consulting his cabinet or in opposition to the views of his cabinet. Granted, however, that the Queen's representative must act only on the advice of a Prime Minister, the question arises, whether or not this means the Prime Minister for the time being. Must the advice of the existing Prime Minister be taken, or is it legitimate for the Queen's representative to refuse to accept this advice and to seek another Prime Minister who might be able to form a government and continue in office without a dissolution? Opinions differ on this matter. Some argue that the power of dissolution is now, by convention, in the hands of the Prime Minister for the time being and that he can obtain a dissolution when he pleases. Others argue that there is a discretion vested in the Queen's representative and that it is permissible for him to refuse a dissolution to the Prime Minister for the time being if an alternative Prime Minister can be found who can form a stable government. It was upon this principle that Sir Patrick Duncan, the Governor-General of South Africa, acted in 1939 when he refused a dissolution to General Hertzog upon his defeat in parliament and appointed General Smuts to succeed him as Prime Minister. General Smuts had a majority behind him and no dissolution occurred. These are controversial matters and it would be difficult to reduce such usages or conventions as regulate them to any precise form of words.

An interesting example of the transfer of legal power by convention to other hands is found in the working of those provisions in the Constitution of the United States which regulate the way in which the President and Vice-President are elected. The legal power to elect is in the hands of Colleges of Electors chosen in each State by such methods as the legislature of the State determines. By convention, however, these electors exercise no discretion. Their power to choose has in fact passed to the party organizations which decide who the candidates are to be and to the voters who determine, within the procedure laid down by the law, which of these candidates is to be chosen. The Colleges of Electors are no more than a statistical record of the voters' choice. It is true that this result has not been brought about by convention alone; there is a considerable element of legal sanction behind it, varying in extent from State to State. But convention, sanctioned by the whole strength of the party organization, plays a most important part.

The United States provides another example of the way in which convention transfers legal powers in practice from one person to another. By the terms of the Constitution the President has a considerable power of appointment. He exercises this power himself in regard to the highest appointments, unlike the head of a state in which a system of cabinet government obtains. But in regard to most other appointments his power is practically transferred by the operation of a convention which is usually called 'senatorial courtesy'. There is an understanding that the senators of the President's own party have the right to advise him upon appointments to posts under the United States which fall vacant in their respective States, and that the President will usually accept their nominations. Should there be no senators of the same party as the President from a particular State, the President will usually accept the nominations of his party's officials and leaders in that State. By this means the presidential power of appointment to a wide range of offices is transferred from the President himself to party leaders and particularly to senators.

Usage and convention change Constitutions in yet another way. They supplement the law. Powers granted in law to some person or institution are exercised in fact by that institution—they are not nullified or transferred by convention—but they carry the matter part of the way only. To understand fully how the matter is regulated, usage and convention must be brought into the picture. An obvious example of the supplementing of the law of the Constitution by convention is found in the standing orders of legislatures. Powers to legislate are conferred upon two houses, but the way in which these powers will be exercised is determined by standing orders. Thus the committee system of the French parliament under the Fourth Republic was established not in the Constitution but in the standing orders of the chambers—as was the case of their predecessors, the Chamber of Deputies and the Senate, under the Third Republic. This committee system was of the greatest importance in French government—it affected the powers of the cabinet and went far to account for the relative weakness of French cabinets. In particular the rule that a bill must be considered by a committee before it obtained the approval of the Assembly placed the government in a weak position, for it was open to a committee to propose what changes it thought fit in the bill.

The significance of these arrangements in France can be judged if we look at the different system which operates, again by conventions, expressed in the form of standing orders, in the parliamentary systems of the British Commonwealth, which have been modelled on the parliament of the United Kingdom. In these British systems standing orders provide that a bill shall not be considered in committee until it has been approved, on a second reading, by the house. In this way action in committee can be confined to attempts to amend the bill in detail, but not in principle, for the principles have already been accepted by the house. The merits of the two systems are open to debate. What is significant for us is that by convention the whole balance of power in the legislative process in a country can be affected. The law of the Constitution is supplemented by conventions which give it a new meaning. The legislative process cannot be understood in these countries without taking into account these conventions as well as the law.

The composition of a cabinet in some countries is regulated or influenced by usage and convention. When a President of the United States is appointing members to his cabinet he has in law practically unfettered power to appoint whom he will. But by usage, at least, he tries to ensure that all his appointments will not be made from, say, the eastern States alone or the middle-western States alone. He will try to spread the appointments so that the main regions of the United States to which he attaches political importance will get some representation. It is difficult to express this in terms of a rule, yet it is probably true to say that by convention he tries to introduce some element of federation into his cabinet.

The principle seems even more firmly established in Australia and Canada. In Australia it is accepted that, if at all possible, each of the six States should have some representation in the Cabinet of the Commonwealth. Though this may not always happen, there is a feeling that it should be done and that there has been some breach of faith which requires justification and explanation if it is not done. In Canada some rules can be laid down with complete assurance and the first and most binding of all is that there must be French- and English-speaking Canadians in a Canadian Cabinet and that Quebec must be represented. Secondly each of the ten Canadian provinces must, if at all possible, have at least one representative in the Cabinet. Then there is a usage, probably a convention, that Quebec and Ontario must have approximately equal representation; that the Protestant minority in Quebec should be represented in the Cabinet; that English-speaking Catholics, probably outside Quebec, should be represented, and that the French Canadians outside Quebec shall not be overlooked. Obviously these arrangements are not always all possible at the same time, but there are strong pressures which tend to make them obligatory. In this way, in Canada as in Australia, usage and convention supplement the law of the Constitution which usually does little more than provide in outline for an institution through which executive power is to be exercised. This outline is of course supplemented also by statutory provisions establishing ministries and organizing departments, but usage and convention supplement the Constitution, too, in the ways outlined above.

An interesting comparison of the way in which convention operates to supplement the law of a Constitution is found when we consider the difference in the status and function of the Speaker in the American House of Representatives and in, say, the Canadian House of Commons. The Constitution makes practically identical provision in each case, giving to each House the power to elect a Speaker, but saying very little about his powers and duties. Convention has operated to make the Speaker of the American House the principal leader of the majority party in the House, whereas in Canada he is almost the complete reverse of this. The American Speaker is an active organizer of his party's legislative programme; he performs indeed many of the functions which a Prime Minister or Leader of the House of Commons would perform in the United Kingdom, in Canada, or in any country which has a system of cabinet government. The Canadian Speaker, though not so far removed from politics as the Speaker of the House of Commons in the United Kingdom, approaches closely to that model. Convention regulates the office still further in Canada, for there is an understanding that the speakership will alternate in successive parliaments between a French-speaking and an English-speaking member, and there is a further provision, embodied in standing orders, that if the Speaker is French-speaking, the Deputy Speaker must be English-speaking and vice-versa. In all the countries of the British Commonwealth the office of Speaker is regulated, to a greater or less degree, by usage and convention. There is a good deal of variety in detail from place to place, but there is one point upon which all are agreed—the party leader could not combine the Speakership with leadership of his party.

It cannot be stressed too often that usage and convention must not be considered in isolation from the law of the Constitution. They operate upon each other, and neither can be effective without the other. The line drawn between them, too, is often fine and it is sometimes difficult to decide whether some particular matter should be embodied in the law of the Constitution or whether it should be left to regulation by usage and convention. A good illustration of this point is found in Switzerland. The Constitution provides that no two members of the Federal Council—a body of seven persons—may come from the same Canton. Here the law of the Constitution regulates the sort of matter which in Canada and Australia, for example, is left entirely to usage and convention. But convention plays its part in Switzerland, too, for it is understood that the three Cantons of Berne, Zurich, and Vaud will always be represented in the Council, and also that not more than five of the seven members will be chosen from the German-speaking Cantons. Thus the composition of the Federal Council is adjusted to the problems of minority rights by a combination of the law of the Constitution and convention.

It is interesting to find, moreover, that matters which in one country are regulated substantially by usage and convention are in others regulated by law. Conventions are, indeed, not only reduced to writing but also enacted as part of the Constitution. Thus not all countries which have adopted the cabinet system of executive, have been content to leave the rules which regulate it to statutory law and to custom and usage. In the Constitution of the Republic of Ireland there is a series of provisions (Articles 13 and 28) defining fairly closely the rules which are to regulate the cabinet system. It is provided that the President shall appoint the Prime Minister on the nomination of the Dail, the popularly elected house of the legislature; that the other ministers shall be appointed by the President on the nomination of the Prime Minister but with the previous approval of the Dail; that the Dail shall be summoned and dissolved by the President on the advice of the Prime Minister; that the government is responsible to the Dail; that the Prime Minister shall resign from office upon his ceasing to retain the support of a majority in the Dail unless on his advice the President dissolves the Dail and on the re-assembly of the Dail after the dissolution the Prime Minister secures the support of a majority of the Dail; and that if the Prime Minister resigns from office at any time, the other members of the government shall be deemed to have resigned from office.

There are provisions on like matters of detail in the Constitution of the Fifth French Republic. In an attempt to remove some of the causes of cabinet instability, provisions have been inserted to regulate the committee systems of the legislature—a matter which was left to standing orders under the Third and Fourth Republics, as was mentioned earlier. Article 43 limits the number of permanent standing committees to six for each assembly—there were nineteen under the Fourth Republic. If the government wishes, bills are to be sent to *ad hoc* committees, not to the permanent committees. Moreover, by Article 42, when government bills are discussed, the text is to be the government's text, not that of the committee.

Detailed provision is made for votes of confidence in Article 49. The Prime Minister, after deliberation in the Council of Ministers, pledges the responsibility of the government before the National Assembly on its programme or, if it be so decided, on a general declaration of policy. The National Assembly challenges the responsibility of the government by passing a vote of censure. A censure motion is in order only if it is signed by at least one tenth of the members of the National Assembly. The vote may not take place until 48 hours after its introduction. Only votes in favour of the censure motion are counted, and the motion is carried only if it receives the votes of the majority of the members of the Assembly. And Article 50 provides that when the National Assembly passes a motion of censure or rejects the government's programme or general statement of government policy, the Prime Minister must tender to the President of the Republic the resignation of the government.

The close connexion between usage and convention on the one hand and the law of the Constitution on the other is illustrated further when we encounter cases where a convention is turned into law, perhaps by being embodied through amendment in the Constitution itself. This is thought to be necessary perhaps because the law is regarded, in some cases, as having a stronger sanction than convention. Or it may be that a convention is disputed and it is thought best to settle the dispute by enacting the rule. Or it may be that the convention is impeded by the law and if it is to be effective requires the alteration of the law, for it must always be remembered that though a convention may nullify the exercise of legal powers or transfer them or supplement them, it can never abolish them or amend them. The limb may be paralysed but it cannot be amputated except by the processes of the law itself.

An interesting example of this process is found in the attempt in the United States, after President Franklin Roosevelt's death, to amend the Constitution so that it should be illegal for a President to stand for re-election for a third full term of office. This attempt, which began in January 1947, issued in the Twenty-Second Amendment of the Constitution, finally adopted in February 1951. It was evidently felt that there was doubt about the rule which did apply in the matter of re-election and also that there must be applied the legal sanction of the Constitution which no convention could overcome. It is sometimes suggested, too, that some of the rules which regulate the relations between the Queen's representative and ministers in the countries of the British Commonwealth should be regulated by provisions in the Constitution or that powers which, by convention, have been nullified, should be removed.

Convention can become law also by judicial recognition. In the ordinary law of the land it is often within the province of Courts to recognize customs, under certain conditions, as part of the law. The same thing is possible in constitutional law. When a convention is so recognized it becomes a part of the law; it is no longer a convention. Such recognition is rare, however, and it is obviously fraught with some danger. By what tests can a Court decide that a custom or convention is ripe for recognition? What evidence can it call to establish precisely either the terms of the convention or its antiquity or its authority?

It is interesting to ask in conclusion whether there is any general trend in the operation of usage and convention in countries which carry out their government under a Constitution. This is not an easy question to answer. There is, however, one characteristic which is found in many examples of the working of convention, a characteristic which Dicey described in his *Law of the Constitution* when he said of conventions in the British system of government that they were 'intended to secure the ultimate supremacy of the electorate as the true political soveriegn of the state'. This description of the effect of conventions applies to many countries besides Britain. When the power of veto of the head of the state is nullified, or when the electoral colleges of the United States cease to have any discretion to elect a President, we see the development of rules which are intended to remove obstacles from the giving effect to the will of the people. The point is illustrated in a different way when we ask why, if convention has nullified the veto power of a King in a European country or in the British Commonwealth, the veto power of the President of the United States has not been nullified also. The answer would seem to be that the President is elected by the people and he may claim the right to express their will as much as Congress can. Had the American President continued to be elected indirectly by the electoral colleges in practice as the law of the Constitution intended, it may well be that his veto power would have been greatly restricted, if not nullified, by convention. The explanation of the survival and indeed extended use of the President's veto power is, of course, more complicated than this, but the fact of his election by the people is certainly relevant to it.

But it will have been clear from what has been said in this chapter that usage and convention regulate a wider sphere than this. They provide safeguards for minority rights, as in Switzerland or Canada; they regulate relations between the two houses of a legislature; they govern the internal organization of a legislature and in so doing can affect profoundly the position of the executive and its relation with the legislature; they link the force of party with the legal institutions of government and in so doing may transform its nature and alter its balance of power. They can provide flexibility and change when recourse to the machinery of formal amendment might be premature, inopportune, or even disastrous; they can bring changes which the law cannot comprehend. Yet it is always well to remember that they, too, have their limits. They cannot accomplish all things. They may postpone and alleviate but they cannot finally obviate difficulties with which only formal amendment or judicial interpretation are competent to deal.

9

Prospects for Constitutional Government

CONSTITUTIONAL GOVERNMENT means something more than government according to the terms of a Constitution. It means government according to rule as opposed to arbitrary government; it means government limited by the terms of a Constitution, not government limited only by the desires and capacities of those who exercise power. It might happen, therefore, that although government in a particular country was conducted according to the terms of the Constitution, that Constitution did no more than establish the institutions of government and leave them free to act as they wished. In such a case we would hardly call the government constitutional government. The real justification of Constitutions, the original idea behind them, is that of limiting government and of requiring those who govern to conform to law and rules. Most Constitutions, as we have seen, do purport to limit the government. Before we can conclude, however, that a country which has a Constitution limiting the government, has also constitutional government, we must see how the Constitution works in practice, and see in particular whether usage and convention operate to strengthen or to weaken constitutional limitations. In the same way we cannot conclude that a country lacks constitutional government simply because its Constitution appears to impose no limitations on the government; it may well be that further study will show that the ordinary law of the land combined with usage and convention supply those checks which the law of the Constitution did not.

Is it possible to form some opinion, in the light of our previous chapters, of the prospects of constitutional government in this sense?

It would be foolish to prophesy. It is possible, however, to say with reasonable certainty which forces operate against constitutional government, to weaken and destroy it. The reader can speculate how strong these forces may be.

A first force which works against constitutional government is war. In time of war or of rumours of war, a government claims full freedom of action; it does not want to be bound by limitations. People are usually ready to grant this freedom. Obviously government on these lines is opposed to the limited government which we call constitutional. The extent to which constitutional government has been suspended in time of war varies a great deal. It need not be assumed that war means the destruction of constitutional government in every case. Yet it is certain to put a strain upon it and it usually suspends it in some degree. Constitutions themselves recognize this almost inevitable consequence of war by the provisions which most of them contain allowing freedom to the government in time of war or in defence of the public safety. The words of Article 28(3) of the Irish Constitution are typical of many: 'Nothing in this Constitution shall be invoked to invalidate any law enacted by the legislature which is expressed to be for the purpose of securing the public safety and the preservation of the State in time of war or armed rebellion. . . .' Put in simple language it means that a Constitution and with it constitutional government may be suspended in time of war.

War is just one example—if the extreme example—of a state of crisis or emergency which causes and justifies the suspension of constitutional government. Economic distress or difficulty, famine, pestilence, disaster all in some degree call for discretionary action by government. They lead to the suspension of the ordinary limitations upon government in order to permit swift and effective action. Crisis or emergency government can seldom be constitutional government. Peace and prosperity are in truth strong allies of constitutional government. Their prospects are its prospects.

If constitutional government is limited government, it follows that one of its enemies is absolutism of any kind. Any body of opinion and any organized movement which aims at establishing omnipotent government is clearly a force opposed to constitutional government. Absolutism appears under many names and forms—it may be called totalitarian, dictatorship of the proletariat, fascism, or nazi-ism, and it may be enshrined in a Constitution, but it is incompatible with constitutional government because it claims to be unlimited and supreme. The prospects of constitutional government depend therefore on the strength of absolutism in its various forms. As it advances, constitutional government recedes. In the middle of the twentieth century two thirds of the world's population lives under some form of absolute government.

Can it be concluded, then, that democracy is an essential prerequisite of constitutional government? If democracy means no more than universal suffrage or equality of conditions, it does not follow at all that it will produce constitutional government. Universal suffrage can create and support a tyranny of the majority or of a minority or of one man. De Tocqueville said, in his *Democracy in Amreica*, that 'it is easier to establish an absolute and despotic government among a people in which the conditions of society are equal, than among any other'. The absolutisms of the twentieth century have usually been based upon universal suffrage—and a compulsory universal suffrage at that. Have not modern tyrannies been returned to power by majorities of over 90 per cent?

It is only if democracy means liberty as well as equality that it can be expected with any confidence to produce constitutional government. If men are free not only to vote but also to vote for an alternative government to that in power, and if their rights even against the State itself are secured, then there is a chance that limited government may exist. In a democracy men often love equality more than liberty, and if need be they will throw away liberty to secure equality. If democratic government is to be constitutional government, it must preserve liberty. Democracy, as it is understood in the United States and in the countries of the British Commonwealth, for example, does signify liberty and indeed places liberty first, even before equality itself if it has to choose. In these countries democratic government and constitutional government are thought of as almost the same thing.

It is important to notice, however, that while democratic government, as understood in Anglo-Saxon countries, may be also constitutional government, it is possible to find examples of constitutional government which are not democratic. Aristocracy and oligarchy can be examples of constitutional government. Government controlled by a class, though operated in the interests of that class, may easily be limited government. A belief in weak govrenment is often found among aristocracies. The Constitution of the United States was the product of an oligarchic society and the government it set up was limited in the ways which the ruling minority favoured. Democracy appeared to the framers of that Constitution as mob rule or majority tyranny which would sweep away all the checks upon government. Constitutional government is not synonymous with democratic government, therefore, whether the latter be conceived of either as the exercise of universal suffrage and no more or as limited free government.

To those who value constitutional government in modern times, however, the problem which confronts them most is how to ensure that democratic government will be constitutional government. It is useless to attempt to establish constitutional government by a return to aristocracy. 'I am persuaded,' said de Tocqueville, 'that all who shall attempt, in the ages upon which we are entering, to base freedom upon aristocratic privilege, will fail. . . . The question is not how to reconstruct aristocratic society, but how to make liberty proceed out of that democratic state of society in which God has placed us.'

Perhaps the most difficult problem that confronts constitutional government in modern times is how to defend itself successfully against its enemies and still survive. When war or any other emergency comes, constitutional government is restricted or suspended in order that a community may survive as an independent entity free to choose once more to resume constitutional government when the emergency has passed. Such a suspension of constitutional government is justified on the ground that if it is to exist again in the future, it must be in abeyance for the present. There is nothing theoretically wrong in this. Human beings can understand that it may be necessary for them to submit themselves to supreme authority today, if they are to survive to enjoy freedom tomorrow. The danger in practice is that those to whom supreme authority has been confided may be reluctant to deliver it up. Temporary dictatorship may become an established and permanent tyranny. When the safeguards of constitutional government are delivered up to the rulers, the means of getting them back have been delivered up also.

An even greater problem is presented, however, by the attacks which are made upon constitutional government by those who desire to overthrow it and use the freedom and the liberties which it gives to carry out their campaign against it. Is it compatible with constitutional government to suppress those who work against it? People differ in their answers to this question. Some say that constitutional government means liberty to criticize the form of government and to organize opposition to it, and that to deny this right even to those whose avowed purpose is to do away with constitutional government, is itself a suspension or restriction of constitutional government. Yet it may be doubted whether in principle this argument is sound. Surely it cannot be consistent with constitutional government to tolerate or encourage those who are opposed to it. It may well be that in certain circumstances the best way to defeat the opponents of constitutional government or to restrict their activities is to leave them free to express their opposition. That is a matter of practical politics, and it involves questions requiring a most delicate judgement and most tactful handling. Yet it must always be maintained that the object before the supporters of constitutional government is to defeat its opponents and it may be that their freedom must be surrendered, if constitutional government is to survive.

The difficulties which arise when this principle is applied in practice are illustrated by the attempts made in countries under constitutional government to suppress the activities of Communists. In theory there is no inconsistency between constitutional government and suppression of Communists. Communists do not believe in constitutional government and they do not hide their contempt for it. Yet if they are to be apprehended or dislodged from positions of influence or rendered harmless, very wide powers have to be conferred upon the government, powers which have to be exercised swiftly and secretly. One underground movement must be opposed by another. Powers of this kind may easily be abused. Citizens are placed in jeopardy by the unfounded charges of their enemies and rivals; spying and lying are encouraged and rewarded; the ordinary safeguards of a fair trial are in suspense. All these things, so contrary to constitutional government, are liable to arise when such a government attempts to defend itself against its enemies. And it is in countries where these enemies are strongest that these abuses often are most likely to flourish.

This issue is perhaps the most critical that faces constitutional government in these days. It may be stated shortly in words which Abraham Lincoln used, on 4 July 1861, in his first message to the United States Congress after the outbreak of the Civil War:

It presents to the whole family of man the question whether a constitutional republic or democracy—a government of the people by the same people—can or cannot maintain its territorial integrity against its own domestic foes. It presents the question whether discontented individuals, too few in numbers to control administration according to organic law in any case, can always, upon the pretences made in this case or any other pretences, or arbitrarily without any pretence, break up their government and thus practically put an end to free government upon the earth. It forces us to ask: 'Is there, in all republics, this inherent and fatal weakness? Must a government, of necessity, be too strong for the liberties of its own people, or too weak to maintain its own existence?'

Select Bibliography
Revised 1971

1. The raw materials upon which the student of Constitutions may base his study have been collected from time to time in books of documents. There is Amos J. Peaslee's *Constitutions of Nations*, revised third edition, Vol. 1 *Africa*, 1965; Vol. 2 (in two parts) *Asia, Australia & Oceania*, 1966; Vol. 3 (in two parts) *Europe*, 1968; Vol. 4 (in two parts) *Americas*, 1970, published by Martinus Nijhoff, The Hague. For those interested in Colonial Constitutions, Martin Wight's *British Colonial Constitutions* (Clarendon Press, Oxford, 1951) should be consulted, more particularly for its penetrating and lucid Introduction. Among other collections which repay study are Russell H. Fitzgibbon, *Constitutions of the Americas* (Chicago University Press, 1948); *Les Constitutions Européenes*, by B. Mirkine-Guetzévitch (Presses Universitaires de France, Paris, 2 vols., 1951); *Les Constitutions modernes*, by F. Dareste (Librairie du Recueil Sirez, Paris, 6 vols., 1928–34); A. P. Newton, *Federal and Unified Constitutions* (Longmans, London, 1923); W. F. Dodd, *Modern Constitutions* (Chicago University Press, 2 vols., 1902); L. Wolf-Phillips (ed.), *Constitutions of Modern States* (Pall Mall Press, London, 1968).

2. Many books have been written about the making and working of Constitutions. It is invidious to select, but the reader will find something of value in the following: James Bryce, *Modern Democracies* (Macmillan & Co., London, 2 vols., 1921); J. A. R. Marriott, *The Mechanism of the Modern State* (Oxford University Press, 2 vols., 1927); A. Headlam-Morley, *The New Democratic Constitutions of Europe* (Oxford University Press, 1928); Arnold Zurcher (ed.), *Constitutions and Constitutional Trends since World War II* (New York University Press, 1951, 2nd edn., 1955); J. A. Corry and H. J. Abraham, *Elements of Democratic Government* (Oxford University

Press, New York, 1958); K. C. Wheare, *Federal Government* (Oxford University Press, London, 4th edn., 1963); R. L. Watts, *New Federations: Experiments in the Commonwealth* (Oxford University Press, 1966); S. A. de Smith, *The New Commonwealth and its Constitutions* (Stevens, London, 1964); B. A. Arneson, *The Democratic Monarchies of Scandinavia* (Van Nostrand, New York, 2nd edn., 1949); N. Andrén, *Modern Swedish Government* (Alquist & Wicksell, 2nd edn., 1968); W. E. Rappard, *The Government of Switzerland* (Van Nostrand, New York, 1936), and *La Constitution fédérale de la Suisse, 1848–1948* (Éditions de la Baconnière, Boudry, Neuchâtel, 1948); C. J. Hughes, *The Federal Constitution of Switzerland* (Clarendon Press, Oxford, 1954); W. R. Sharp, *The Government of the French Republic* (Van Nostrand, New York, 1938); P. Williams, *Crisis and Compromise* (Longmans, London, 1965); P. Campbell and B. Chapman, *The Constitution of the Fifth Republic* (Blackwell, Oxford, 2nd edn., 1959); Carl B. Swisher, *The Growth of Constitutional Power in the United States* (Chicago University Press, 1946); R. McG. Dawson, *The Government of Canada* (University of Toronto Press, 4th edn., 1963); G. Austin, *The Indian Constitution* (Clarendon Press, Oxford, 1966); P. B. Mukharji, *The Critical Problems of the Indian Constitution* (Bombay University, 1968).

3. While the books mentioned above deal in a general way with most of the aspects of the working of the Constitutions they treat, it is worth while to consult some of the more specialized studies which consider particular aspects of the subject. On the process of formal constitutional amendment the reader may consult W. S. Livingston, *Federalism and Constitutional Change* (Clarendon Press, Oxford, 1956), L. B. Orfield, *Amending the Federal Constitution* (Michigan University Press, 1942); P. Gerin-Lajoie, *Constitutional Amendment in Canada* (University of Toronto Press, 1950); and the current issue of *The Book of the States* (published by the Council of State Governments in the United States) for details of the procedures used in amending American State Constitutions. The subject of judicial review may be studied in Robert K. Carr, *The Supreme Court and Judicial Review* (Farrar & Rinehart, Inc., New York, 1942); R. B. McCloskey, *The American Supreme Court* (Chicago University Press, 1960); C. H. Pritchett, *The Roosevelt Court, 1937–47* (Macmillan, New York, 1948) and *Congress versus the Court* (Chicago University Press, 1962); E. S. Corwin, *Total War and the Constitution* (Knopf, New York, 1947); Charles A. Fairman, *American*

Constitutional Decisions (Holt & Co., New York, 1948); B. Schwartz, *American Constitutional Law* (Cambridge University Press, 1955); G. Sawer, *Australian Constitutional Cases* (Law Book Co. of Australasia, Sydney, 1948); G. Marshall, *Parliamentary Sovereignty and the Commonwealth* (Clarendon Press, Oxford, 1957). The operation of usage and convention on the Constitution of the United States is discussed in a stimulating way by H. W. Horwill in *The Usages of the American Constitution* (Oxford University Press, London, 1925). The nature of usage and convention is discussed with penetration by A. V. Dicey, *The Law of the Constitution* (Macmillan, London, 9th edn., by E. C. S. Wade, 1939) and W. I. Jennings, *The Law and the Constitution* (University of London Press, 3rd edn., 1949).

4. Constitutions cannot be understood without some study and reflection upon political theory. The great classical writers need not be enumerated here. Suffice it to say that the reader should study in particular John Locke's *Second Treatise on Civil Government*; Tom Paine's *Rights of Man* and *Common Sense*; and A. Hamilton, J. Jay, and J. Madison's *The Federalist*, probably the greatest book on Constitutions written in English. Among modern writers he might consult H. Kelsen, *General Theory of Law and State* (Harvard University Press, 1945), G. C. Haines, *The Revival of Natural Law Concepts* (Harvard University Press, 1930), C. H. McIlwain, *Constitutionalism and the Changing World* (Cambridge University Press, 1939) and *Constitutionalism: Ancient and Modern* (Cornell University Press, 1940), M. J. C. Vile, *Constitutionalism and the Separation of Powers* (Clarendon Press, Oxford, 1967).

Index